PRAISE FOR

RETIREMENT
STEPPING STONES

"Retirement is extremely complex and continues to change. People need guidance and a process. They need to be able to understand the hurdles that are in front of them and ways they cannot just survive retirement but actually thrive in it and leave a meaningful legacy. This book walks you through the hurdles and roadblocks that can be in your way and provides a streamlined and easy-to-follow process so you can leave a life-changing legacy at the end of your retirement."

—Jamie P. Hopkins, Esq., MBA, CFP®, LLM, CLU®, ChFC®, RICP®, managing partner of Wealth Solutions, Carson Group, author of *Rewirement: Rewiring the Way You Think About Retirement!*

"It is evident that Tony Hixon cares deeply about helping others. He's taken a tragic story and turned it into a learning opportunity for the world to benefit from. This book has made me rethink how I view work, retirement, and long-term planning. I'm grateful for Tony's courage to write it."

—Ryan Hawk, host of *The Learning Leader Show* and author of the best-selling book *Welcome to Management: How to Grow from Top Performer to Excellent Leader*

"This book offers a path to retirement that goes beyond the facts and figures to get to the heart of planning, using our capital to live a life that's meaningful. It's time to redefine retirement, and this personal yet practical read offers an unexpectedly poignant view of how working with a trusted advisor can help you do just that with greater purpose and peace of mind."

—**Stephanie Bogan,** founder & CEO of Limitless Advisor

"In this deeply moving, relevant book, Tony exposes the smoldering discontent that is so common, yet often overlooked, in seasons of transition. Through personal reflection and practical tips, he highlights the opportunity we each have to turn stumbling blocks into stepping-stones on our unique paths to finishing well."

—**Dean Niewolny,** chairman of Halftime Institute and author of *Trade Up: How to Move from Just Making Money to Making a Difference*

"God wastes nothing. Even Tony's mother taking her own life. Out of this tragedy, Tony has integrated truths that most of us don't connect. The relationship between purpose, transition, identity, and finances. Strange but essential bedfellows. This is a book that should be read slowly . . . and before you think you need it. You and the people around you will be better for it."

—**Gary Harpst,** founder and CEO of Six Disciplines and author of *The New York Times* and *Wall Street Journal* best-selling book *Six Disciplines® Execution Revolution*

"Tony has done an incredible job of intertwining vulnerability and practicality. In his unique voice, this story will inspire the reader to do more than just the status quo. It is clear to me that, as someone in my 40s, this isn't about racing towards retirement, but rather it is about finding a deeper meaning to serve the world abroad. As culture continues to feel more and more vague, this is a resource to help us get focused—no matter what age."

—**Reverend Tony Miltenberger,** lead pastor of Restoration Church and host of *Reclamation Podcast*

"For many people, the prospect of retirement is exciting—the just reward of a life well lived and the long-awaited result of responsible decision-making. But this is not true for everyone. Tony Hixon uses a personal tragedy he's experienced to educate us about the softer side of financial planning. Numbers can be made to fit on a spreadsheet and may sometimes offer us comfort about the future. But that's only the beginning of the process."

—**Downtown Josh Brown,** CEO of Ritholtz Wealth Management, on-air contributor to CNBC, and author of *How I Invest My Money: Finance Experts Reveal How They Save, Spend and Invest*; *Clash of the Financial Pundits: How the Media Influences Your Investment Decisions for Better or Worse*; *Backstage Wall Street: An Insider's Guide to Knowing Who to Trust, Who to Run From, and How to Maximize Your Investments*

"A meaningful retirement requires more than a focus on finances. *Retirement Stepping Stones* offers a step-by-step road map for planning a purposeful, engaging, and enjoyable second act of life. Reading this book will help inspire and equip you with the tools needed to live your best life."

—**Nancy Collamer,** founder of MyLifestyleCareer.com and author of *Second-Act Careers: 50+ Ways to Profit from Your Passions in Retirement*

RETIREMENT
STEPPING STONES

FIND MEANING, LIVE WITH PURPOSE, AND LEAVE A LEGACY

TONY HIXON

WITH FOREWORD BY ADAM ZUERCHER

RIVER GROVE
BOOKS

This book is intended as a reference volume only. It is sold with the understanding that the publisher and author are not engaged in rendering any professional services. The information given here is designed to help you make informed decisions. If you suspect that you have a problem that might require professional treatment or advice, you should seek competent help.

Published by River Grove Books
Austin, TX
www.rivergrovebooks.com

Distributed by River Grove Books

Design and composition by Greenleaf Book Group
Cover design by Greenleaf Book Group
Cover Image: Alistair Berg / DigitalVision / Getty Images

Publisher's Cataloging-in-Publication data is available.

Print ISBN: 978-1-63299-403-5

eBook ISBN: 978-1-63299-404-2

Audiobook ISBN: 978-1-63299-405-9

First Edition

To Eliana, Kya, and Everett,
may this story inspire you to never give up.

In life you will encounter stumbling blocks.
Turn them into stepping-stones.
And may you come to realize, as I have,
that the best is ahead . . .
always.

CONTENTS

FOREWORD

My name is Adam Zuercher, and I cofounded Hixon Zuercher Capital Management with Tony in 2002. Few people realize that Tony and I actually went to high school together in a little town outside of Findlay, Ohio. At the time, we never would have imagined starting a business together or even the fact that we both would go into the field of financial planning. We were just two kids trying to figure life out.

We lost touch in the years following high school, as I think many kids do. It wasn't until after we had both graduated from college and started our careers that we reconnected. Tony and I had both graduated with degrees in accounting and were working for two local firms in the greater Findlay, Ohio, area. In an effort to reconnect and network a little bit within our field, we started going to lunch together pretty regularly. It was a breath of fresh air to catch up with someone I had known for so long, especially as the nation and the financial industry were going through such turbulent times. The markets were still recovering from the tech bubble, and after the tragedy of 9/11, our meetings started to shift from casual lunches to strategy sessions.

Those lunches were the foundation of the business we currently run today. Together, we realized that entrepreneurship was something we both wanted in our future. This idea was partially born out of a shared desire to start something of our own and to embrace the many benefits that come with launching a business—a flexible schedule, more time with our families, and a sense of accomplishment and ownership. However, we also shared a deeply held belief that we wanted to offer a safe space for people to get relevant, impactful financial advice. Over the years, we had seen many tax clients come through our office during filing season who were making notable financial mistakes. They were almost always either doing their financial plan on their own or had worked with a financial advisor who had given them faulty advice.

Unfortunately, the nature of tax season is that it only lasts for a short period of time. People think about their financial lives when they meet with their CPA to file their returns each year and then check it off their to-do lists. We wanted to be part of something that nurtured people on their journey toward financial freedom in a more comprehensive and ongoing way. Both of us wanted to be a resource for clients year-round, not just during tax season.

Freedom Financial Solutions (renamed Hixon Zuercher Capital Management in 2011) was born from this desire to help others reach their retirement goals. When we started our firm in 2002, we were working in a spare room at my house. We had no clients and no assets under management; we truly were building from the ground up. Over the next few years, we slowly grew our business with the goal of helping people win with their investments. However, we were both admittedly numbers guys. When we worked with clients, our primary focus was whether or not they were going to retire successfully. To us, the definition of success was simple: Our clients wouldn't run out of money during retirement, and their wealth would outlive them. We became incredibly technically proficient in the world of financial planning, and so when Tony's parents came to us to get a second set of eyes on their retirement plan, we were confident.

The numbers added up. Tony's mom could successfully retire, with his dad planning to retire shortly thereafter, with ease. They'd have to continue living within their means, but I remember looking over the numbers with Tony and agreeing that they were ready. It was only months later that Tony's mom, Pam, took her life.

I remember being in the locker room at the gym when I heard the news. I had just finished a workout and was getting ready to come into the office. Checking my phone as I packed up, I saw that I had several missed calls from Tony. Now, Tony's not the kind of guy who calls. Typically, we shoot text messages back and forth. I immediately was uneasy. Multiple missed calls? I called him back, and he told me what had happened.

To say I was shocked doesn't even begin to cover how I felt.

Depression is a disease that warps how the mind perceives reality. While I had been somewhat aware of Tony's mom's mental-health struggles since retiring, it was still jarring that her depression and anxiety had escalated so quickly. After all, she had retired less than six months earlier. It felt unfair, like this new chapter in her life hadn't even started to unfold before it was cut short. Although I felt helpless to remedy a broken situation, I also knew that this was something Tony, or anyone else in his mother's life, couldn't have predicted. The change in Pam had happened so rapidly, it seemed like everyone in her world was reeling from the abrupt way her story ended.

One thing that later solidified in my own mind was that our financial-planning process needed to shift. Although numbers will always be the foundation of what we do, like Tony, I recognized the need for intentional coaching in our work. We started to look more closely at how our firm could approach retirement planning with a dynamic mind-set. Even if we prioritized the financial component of someone's plan, we wanted to ensure we opened the door to tough conversations about lifestyle, mental health, and the retirement transition.

Our work at Hixon Zuercher Capital Management, and the work of this book, is one of the many ways we're actively trying to honor Tony's mom. Her story is tragic, but she was the type of woman who wouldn't want her tragedy to be someone else's narrative as well. My hope for this book is that Tony, and, by extension, our business, can help educate and empower others to plan for a fulfilling and joyful retirement. The core of our business has always been a desire to help and serve others. In my mind, there's no better way to do that than to approach retirement planning with a holistic and comprehensive process. We've always been a people-first firm, and this tragic event has spurred us to lean in and continue to prioritize the well-being of our clients in the work we do.

PROLOGUE—MY STORY

Sometimes, unexpected events have a lifelong impact not only on our day-to-day lives but also on the way we see the world and how we relate to others in our lives—family, friends, and those we do business with. Something like that happened to me, and one result is the book you're reading.

I've been a financial planner and business owner since 2002, although entrepreneurship was never originally in my plan. In fact, when I grew up on a farm outside of Findlay, Ohio, all I knew was that I wanted to get out into the world and do something with numbers. Math had always been a strong suit of mine. I chose to attend Ohio Northern University, where I earned my bachelor's degree in accounting. After graduating, I started work at a local accounting firm. I loved what I was doing, but I had a feeling that there was something more in store for me.

As passionate as I was about technical financial work (I still am a numbers guy, after all), I was frustrated to see how many people struggled to live comfortably throughout their retirement. The majority of my accounting firm clients had the means to live any lifestyle they wanted, but through a lack of planning, they were struggling. They owed more in taxes than they wanted to and were unable to check off all their bucket-list items during the exact time of their lives when living happily should have been a priority!

I also felt an immense frustration that the clients I was helping were essentially project based. By that, I mean that I'd see them annually during tax season, then they'd disappear until the following year. I consider tax planning a critical component of a comprehensive financial strategy, not a time-to-time activity. Still, I felt like I was helping clients create Band-Aid solutions retroactively to account for past financial mistakes. I wanted to help clients become proactive about their money and empower them to live lives they were proud of, and I was ready to do that.

In 2002 my business partner, Adam Zuercher, and I decided to launch Hixon Zuercher Capital Management. We had originally met back in high school. Of course, as two teenage kids growing up in a small town outside of Findlay, Ohio, we never had imagined we'd be setting out to launch a business together years later. We were both passionate about financial planning and helping our clients reach their goals and retire with confidence. As a self-proclaimed numbers guy, I was eager to give our clients a technical overview of their strategy. We had software that could create long, detailed reports, and I'll admit that I found solace in the certainty that numbers provided. My goal was to help our clients ensure that they wouldn't outlive their money—and possibly even have enough to accomplish some of those bucket-list goals.

However, after several years of doing business with only numbers as my criteria for client success, a family crisis changed my thinking and how I now counsel clients to think about their lives and plan for the future.

My mom, Pam Hixon, came to me when she turned 60. She was eager to retire but wanted to know if she could financially pull it off. I took some time to crunch the numbers for her. She had enough saved to live comfortably, and so I gave her the go-ahead.

Like many people, my mom had built up retirement as an ideal in her mind. She imagined long days of relaxing, filling her hours with her favorite hobbies and activities, and spending more time with her loved ones. She had two granddaughters, and her first grandson was on the way. She wanted to connect more with the kids, and she was ready to travel with my dad, Bob Hixon.

Unfortunately, she didn't have a detailed plan for her retirement lifestyle. There was no way the grand ideas she had focused on before retirement could fill *all* of her time.

As the big day started creeping up on her, my mom started feeling less excited and more anxious. I spent time reviewing the financial data with her, reassuring her that her savings would last and that her projected expenses were well within reason, given the size of her nest egg.

As I kept talking to her, I realized that her anxiety wasn't completely financially rooted. "Are you sure you want to do this?" I asked her. She insisted she was, though she admitted she was a bit concerned. She wasn't sure what would come next. Still, she was burned out at her job, and I and many of my family members thought that getting out from under the pressure of work would free her up to live more joyfully.

She retired almost as soon as I gave her the green light in 2010. What happened next changed my life and the direction of my career.

Previously, when working with clients, I had seen only the rosy side of retirement. These folks were excited to enter the next chapter of their lives and had a clear idea about how they wanted to spend their time as retirees. I believe my mom was the first person I spoke to who actually felt unsettled by the idea of leaving her career. She wasn't sure what the next chapter looked like, and she wasn't particularly open to putting a plan together for both her finances *and* her lifestyle.

But now I know exactly how necessary that is for

pre-retirees. These days our wealth management firm focuses on the quantitative financial data *and* the softer, nonfinancial side of retirement when meeting with our clients. We talk to them seriously about the possibility that, when they retire, they may feel lost.

It's a sad truth that your chance of suffering from depression goes up by close to 40 percent after you retire, and approximately 25 percent of adults[1] over age 65 are experiencing some form of mental-health issue. The worst part is that very few people openly discuss this increasingly problematic issue. Retirement is still painted as 20-plus years of vacation. As a result, retirees are underprepared to face their retirement in an empowered way that allows them to live into their purpose.

Pam Hixon's Legacy

Part of my mission now is to carry on the legacy of my mom. I firmly believe that, although her life story ended in tragedy, it doesn't have to stop there. My mom had been dedicated to helping others in every way she could. Now I'm carrying on this tradition in my own work as a financial advisor.

I want to help my clients and loved ones prepare for a

---

1   Kathleen Coxwell, "Retirement Depression: 9 Tips for Combating This Very Common Syndrome," NewRetirement.com, August 29, 2019, https://www.newretirement.com/retirement/retirement-depression.

retirement they love; I'm dedicated to showing them how to build a lifestyle that gives them purpose. Without a plan, life in retirement can lose meaning. My goal, both in my work and now with this book, is to help people who are planning for retirement make that transition with confidence. There's no reason to enter retirement blindly. With a few clear steps, you can build a strategy that helps you derive meaning from your life and add purpose to your days, even as you leave your career behind.

That's the reason for this book. I want to ensure that *your* retirement brings you pleasure, serenity of mind, and the enjoyment of a well-lived life. That your transition is from success to significance. That you find a newfound hope and a newfound purpose. That retirement brings you your best years. My ultimate desire is that your retirement equals peace.

Chapter 1

ONE DAY IN MARCH

Gray. Seemingly the only color of the rainbow. Winter's fury coming to an end. Spring not yet arrived. I'd driven this road for 12 years, back and forth from my office, day after day.

This day, March 22, 2011, was different. This day I specifically noticed how gray it actually was. I hadn't seen the sun in a long time. The grass was still dead. Trees had not yet bloomed. When would the change of seasons come? I was ready.

Twenty-two minutes is the average drive from my house to my office, assuming I hit the traffic lights just right. A man of routine, I walked in, grabbed the paper, and said good morning to Missy at the front desk. She kindly acknowledged my presence as I headed to my desk to start my workday.

I was perusing the front page of the local newspaper when my cell phone began to vibrate at the corner of my desk. I typically don't take calls during the day, but at this particular moment I decided to look up and see who might be calling me. It was Dad.

I answered the phone.

"Hey, Dad."

"Tony!"

Something was wrong. That voice . . . that tone . . . I had never heard him pronounce my name with such intentionality, such furor, such devastation.

"Tony! She did it!"

"She did what?" I questioned.

"She took her life! Pam . . . Mom . . . she committed suicide!"

I struggled to find words.

"I'll be over soon, Dad."

Trembling, I closed the newspaper. My legs gave out as if I were a prizefighter staggering from an uppercut, and I sank to the floor. A stream of emotions overwhelmed me. Shock, denial, anger, guilt. My heart beat rapidly, as if I had just run a race. Beads of sweat gathered on my forehead.

Taking a deep breath, I collected myself, got up, and proceeded to my vehicle. I reached for my phone. I had to call my wife. I wanted to be the one to break the news to Keri.

The gray that permeated the sky now seemed to penetrate my heart. I needed to get to Dad's house. I needed to provide love and support to him. I had to keep it together because I knew he would be falling apart.

The road seemed longer that day. What only took 30 minutes seemed like hours. I needed to cry. No time for that. Push forward. Be strong. Man up.

I remembered the time, years ago, when my Grandpa Hixon died. I was 11 years old then. Old enough to be sad, old enough to remember how Dad remained strong. He didn't cry; he supported us and others through that trying time. Now it was my turn.

The gray road matched the gray sky, which matched my graying heart. Questions began to swirl in my mind . . . How did she do it? Why did she do it? What in the world was she thinking?

When I arrived at my parents' house, I found a police car and another unfamiliar vehicle in the driveway. I pulled in, got out, and tried to take a deep breath . . . but the lump in my throat prevented me from succeeding. I looked at the sky, knowing full well that even in the gray, God was there. He would have to support me through this. Deep down, I knew He would.

I walked in. My dad, 61 years old at the time, had just lost his high school sweetheart who had been his wife for 40 years. The later stages of life that they had hoped, planned, and dreamed for had abruptly come to an end.

I gave him a hug. His body shook. Tears flowed. Moments passed. Words escaped me. Only one word came from his lips . . . over and over . . .

"Why? . . . Why? . . . Why?"

His voice trailed off with each weeping heave.

I didn't have the answer.

Keri soon arrived and joined in the sorrow. Next, my sister, Lynette—known to everyone as Net—and her husband, Mark, arrived. The next several moments were raw.

Emotional.

Painful.

I was angered by the situation.

Hurt.

Lonely.

Unsettled.

In denial.

Guilty.

Moments later, friends and neighbors came to the house to offer their condolences and support. I tried to hold it together as I heard them say over and over again: "Sorry for your loss."

I was sorry, too. What had just happened? How would we piece this all together? She was such a great mom, an awesome grandma.

I began to echo my dad's question . . .

"Why?"

• • •

My checklist began to build, adding more stress to an already stressful situation:

- Make arrangements for the funeral home.

- Write an obituary.

- Purchase a casket.

- Buy and engrave a tombstone.

- Find a burial plot.

So much to do, so little time.

Later that day we found ourselves at the funeral home. The funeral director expressed his condolences to us. Shortly after, he escorted us to the showroom for caskets. I didn't even know such a thing existed. There were all shapes, sizes, colors, and prices. A surreal feeling was turning into reality. I started to lose it.

Why in the world was I shopping for a casket, today of all days? After 12 years of driving to my office, how did I find myself with the family in a showroom for caskets?

One casket in particular, however, stood out to us. On the corners were crosses. Mom's life was centered around her Christian faith, and we thought this would be appropriate for her. "That one," Dad said. "We'll take that one."

Keri and I arrived home that evening knowing full well what we had to do. We needed to tell the kids. We had two daughters at the time. The oldest, Eliana, was four. The youngest, Kya, was three. Questions about how to talk about death with a young child now burdened my heart. How were we supposed to communicate what had happened to their grandma, Mama Pam? How were we to explain that she would no longer be with us? How were we to explain that she had chosen to take her life? What had caused this? How would their young minds understand?

Mom had been such an amazing grandma, showering them with love, gifts, acceptance, and prayers. She loved them with all her heart, and they would miss her greatly. More than they'd even be able to understand at the time.

Sitting down with the girls, I began, "Mama Pam was sick, and she passed away. Now she's in Heaven, and we can celebrate her life." Vague, yet accurate. We knew that someday, when they were older, we'd tell them the full story. But for now, they were still too young to understand.

Two days later I found myself standing in a receiving line at the funeral home. Long lines of people came to pay their respects. That meant hours upon hours of standing, shaking their hands, giving hugs, accepting their condolences. I appreciated each one of them, humbled by the love and support of our friends, family, and community.

Keri stood faithfully by my side in the receiving line. She was seven months pregnant with our third child, a little boy who would be born in May. There was a reprieve from the sadness of the moment when many of the mourners expressed their congratulations for the little one who would soon arrive.

"How far along are you?"

"Is it a boy or a girl?"

The questions I was asking myself, though, were more pointed: "Why, Mom, did you leave two months before he was born? Your first grandson! What an awesome grandma you would have been to him. Why did you do this?"

The line of visitors stretched on, and the condolences continued.

"I'm sorry for your loss."

"You have my sympathy."

"Thank you," I murmured. "Thank you. Thank you."

Throughout the day, I kept trying to get Keri to sit down. I suggested she drink more water and that she get some food. She refused, gave me a hug, smiled, and asked how I was doing. Hours later, we were still greeting those who had come. Later I learned that Keri had been having contractions all day, likely the result of standing far too long and not drinking enough water. But she never left me there alone. She stood by my side, and she still does today. That day, of all days, she lived out our wedding vows: "For better or for worse."

• • •

"Hey, can I talk to you a second?" the funeral attendant motioned me toward a conversation.

"Sure," I replied as we walked a few steps into a private hallway in the funeral home.

"I'm sorry to have to ask you this, but I know your

dad is under a lot of stress right now, and I don't want to bother him with this."

"What is it?" I asked.

"I'm asking you to find a group of pallbearers for the graveside service."

Less than 48 hours after my mom had taken her life, I was being asked to choose a group of men to help carry her casket from the hearse to the grave site.

Pallbearer. What a strange word. A pall is a heavy cloth that is draped over a coffin. Thus, the term "pallbearer" is used to signify someone who bears the coffin that the pall covers. In Western cultures, pallbearers are typically male family members, close friends, or colleagues of the deceased.

As I contemplated what had just been asked, the attendant interrupted, "So can you find some people? If not, I can ask around."

"No, no . . . I mean, yes, I can do that, I can find some guys."

We left the hallway going in different directions. I didn't get far. My knees buckled, and again, a lump in my throat made it hard to swallow. Shaking, I pulled my phone out of my pocket and began to type out a text to my prospective pallbearers. I was sure my voice was too weak to talk.

One by one, the messages arrived back.

"Yes."

"Yes. I'd be honored. I'm so sorry."

"Yes. Can we talk? Love you, brother."

"Yes. Just tell me when and where. I'm here for you, Tony."

"Yes."

And with that, five friends had agreed. Taking a deep breath, I resolved that I would be the sixth. I would help carry my mom's casket to her final resting place.

• • •

The morning was cold, gray, still. Car doors slammed as the graveside service was about to begin. Hundreds had gathered to lay my mom to rest. Sensing that the service was about to begin, I gathered the pallbearers in a circle behind the hearse.

My voice was quivering, yet audible. "Guys, I just wanted to say thank you for agreeing to do this. No one wants to be doing this. This is so unexpected, so crazy, so sad. But I appreciate each one of you. I appreciate our love and our friendship. Know that this coffin isn't the only thing I'm asking you to carry today. Please carry me . . . carry my family. We need your love, support, and prayers right now. It will take time for us to heal. In Sunday school, we're taught to carry each other's burdens. Guys, my burden is heavy. My family's burden is heavy. I'm counting on each of you."

My voice trailed off. No other words were needed. Each of the five offered a hug, acknowledging that they would be there to give me the support and love I needed.

With that, we each assumed our designated positions beside the casket and moved toward the grave site. Physically, the burden was heavy. Emotionally, it was massive.

When the pastor finished his remarks, the crowd returned to their cars, planning to head back to the church for lunch and a continued celebration of Mom's life.

The family was slow to leave, though. We were still trying to take it in. Still trying to make sense of it. Words were sparse and unnecessary. We knew the road ahead was going to be hard. But we knew we had to be strong. I scooped Kya up in my arms and gave her a big kiss. I asked her if she was hungry. "Yes, Daddy!" We all headed back to the car provided by the funeral home to join the others at the church.

Everything happens for a reason.

The points and places we encounter in our lives test our resolve, but I knew I would always choose life and hope. I chose not to allow the tragedy of that day to take me down. It wouldn't take me out. It wouldn't define me. Instead that tragedy moved me to turn that day into triumph.

I resolved that Mom's legacy would live on.

• • •

To understand what happened to my mother, you should know something of her life.

Born on April 11, 1949, in Bluffton, Ohio, Pamela May Frantz graduated from Pandora Gilboa High School and ended up marrying her high school sweetheart, J. Robert Hixon. In 1971 she graduated from college and completed the requirements to become a registered nurse. From there, she went to work at a nearby hospital. She loved caring for others, and that attitude was felt most by my sister and me. Mom worked hard but soon found that the hours and shifts no longer accommodated her family.

When she was offered a home-health nursing job, she was able to be home earlier so she could be there when my sister and I got home from school. The hours were more regular, and as the years progressed, she was able to get another home-health job closer to home, which ultimately led to her interest in hospice nursing.

Hospice programs provide care for the terminally ill. Basically, when normal health care runs out of options, a hospice agency is contacted. Hospice care allows the patient to live out his or her last days in the comfort and familiarity of their own home surrounded by their loving family.

Mom had been promoted at her hospice agency and eventually became the director. It was there that she found fulfillment. It was there that she found her source of strength.

It was there that she achieved the most epic case of burnout I've ever seen.

As a hospice nurse, Mom had worked long and hard hours for years, comforting those who, like it or not, had come to a point where they were forced to make peace with death. She would build relationships not only with the patient but also with the family members who stood by as the patient transitioned from this life to the next.

As family and friends grieved, Mom would show love and support and then move on to the next case. Hour after hour, year after year, the work took a toll on her emotionally, physically, and spiritually. She was done. She wanted—no—she *needed* to retire.

"She was anxious to retire and get out of there," Dad remembers. "They were being forced to computerize, and she didn't love it." The more tech-focused hospice care became, the more my mom found herself behind a computer screen instead of with the patients she cared about.

Mom and Dad had always used another advisor for most of their financial dealings. I felt this was appropriate because we were family, and often family and business don't mix. However, Mom asked me to run some numbers to see if she and Dad would be able to retire soon. She and Dad were excited at the prospect of running my dad's small farm together. They talked about going camping and living a life they loved during retirement.

I sprang into action and whipped my software into shape. The numbers revealed that if they kept a tight control on expenses, Dad continued to work at the factory for a few more years and then continued to farm, they would be fine. Affirming what their other advisor had said, I, too, gave them the green light. And that was that. In the fall of 2010 Mom retired.

For most people, retirement is a time for celebration. A time for exploring, recuperating, and recovering from a career. My mom, though, found herself on Monday morning not quite knowing what to do. She truly had a servant's heart, and when her primary outlet to serve and help others was taken away, she was more than a little lost. She had been so consumed with work that she didn't have many hobbies or outside interests. My dad continued to work, so for long periods of time during the day she was alone. Her friends were also still employed and were not as available as she had hoped.

Fall turned into winter. The grass withered, and the colorful leaves of autumn fell from the trees as nature prepared for a cold season. Sunlight became scarce as clouds filled the sky. Day after day, Mom simply did not have much to do.

She began to lose purpose and then to lose hope. And in a short amount of time, she began to spiral into a deep depression. Dad noticed a shift in Mom's mood. Anxiety seemed to bubble up inside of her in a way it never had before. Lynette remembers my mom sitting on the front steps by her house saying: "I'm not doing well with this." "This," of course, was her transition to retirement. Both my dad and my sister commented on her incessant pacing back and forth. Dad also recalled her sitting in a rocking chair, rocking back and forth obsessively while she worried about money (something that had never before concerned her).

Still, we all assumed that the retirement transition would eventually smooth out.

Over the next several months, she didn't keep quiet about her feelings. She spoke with a counselor, with friends, family, and mentors, and she tried to fill her time with activities she loved. She picked up meditation, focused on prayer, and spent more time with her loved ones. Still, she couldn't shake the feeling of not being needed anymore. After a long and fulfilling career in which she had been an integral part of people's lives, she felt like she no longer brought any value to the world or to the lives of those around her.

The winter was rough. Snow flew, the wind blew, the sun hid, and her depression and anxiety became worse than it had been when she still held her job at the hospice agency.

We knew she wasn't doing well mentally. At the same time, we didn't know how deep the depression truly was. Keri and I would try to go over to my parents' house as often as we could to offer encouragement and ideas for activities to do during the day. But we had our own families and our own jobs. In hindsight, it's now clear we were incapable of providing the deeper support that she needed.

As the depression worsened, Mom reflected on her job as a hospice nurse. When the health care providers felt there was nothing more they could do and stopped treating a patient, they would put the patient into hospice care. As a nurse, she had been there to see that the patient was as comfortable and as much at peace as possible. In the moments before the patient's death, my mom would often be present in the room. She saw patients embrace the fact that their time on earth was fleeting, and she watched them ready themselves for what was next.

But Mom was anything but peaceful. Her prayers didn't seem to be working, and her counselors couldn't understand what she was feeling. She had nowhere to turn.

She thought she had made an epic mistake by retiring. That choice was now her biggest regret. While most retirees enjoy their retirement, she detested the empty hours. Try as she might—with prayer, counseling, songs, sermons, and books—her anxiety snowballed, and her depression deepened.

When she could no longer could stand the emotions that tore at her mind and heart, she felt she had only one option. Her desire for peace of mind became misguidedly intertwined with the peace that she had seen in her patients as they left this world. Ingesting too many sleeping pills, she took the final journey toward the peace she so desired.

The Ripple Effect

The ripple effect through my family and my mom's close-knit community has been profound. As much as her death impacted us, though, it also left us with a deep desire to improve ourselves and our own lives.

Dad was terribly shaken. "I think of her a lot," he says. "Although I try not to think about the past. You learn to compartmentalize." Dad remarried in 2013 and has spent recent years focusing on being better, not bitter. He is a loving husband to his wife, Pat, and continues my mom's legacy of hard work.

My sister was also deeply affected. She and my mom were particularly close, and Net is still jarred thinking that a week before my mom passed away they were baking cookies together and enjoying time as mother and daughter. She now focuses on helping her friends who are nearing retirement find fulfilling ways to spend their time.

As for me personally, I was determined to turn this tragedy—this stumbling block—into a stepping-stone in my life and my career. I wanted to help my other family members, friends, and clients gain a deeper understanding of the implications of retirement. In my work as a client-facing financial advisor, I no longer view retirement through the lens of numbers and software but through the lens of purpose. Over the past decade, I've assisted many people in their transition from career to retirement, and I'm dedicated to making sure that they are mentally, as well as financially, prepared to enjoy their new stage of life. I'm dedicated to ensuring they not only have enough money to sleep at night but enough purpose to get up in the morning.

Journey with me as we navigate these stepping-stones into a life of significance beyond retirement!

Chapter 2

A NEW APPROACH

fter my mom passed away, the approach I took with my financial-planning practice completely changed. Previously, I had "industry blinders" on. Most of the clients who sat across the desk from me were eager to retire. Retirement was the goal, the perfect finish line. The majority of people I spoke with already had big plans to travel, to spend more time with their grandkids, and to enjoy their hobbies.

After talking with them, I was able to punch numbers into our financial-planning software, print out a 32-page document, and confirm whether or not a client was financially ready for retirement. That document and presentation looked good, but after going through such a tragic experience with my family and my loved ones, I realized the financial-planning process didn't go deep enough into what pre-retirees needed to consider in order to determine whether they were truly "ready" to retire. I started implementing a new approach to my conversations with clients.

The firm Adam and I founded, Hixon Zuercher Capital Management,[2] has always been based in Findlay, Ohio. Naturally, we have worked with many clients who live near us, but over the years our vision has grown bigger; technology now enables us to serve clients living anywhere in the United States. In fact, one reason for writing this book is to help more people, people I wouldn't encounter in my own community.

Our goal continues to be to help people retire with financial confidence, and we focus on empowering 50-to-60-year-olds to transition seamlessly. We're experts at crunching the numbers, stress-testing portfolios, and offering advice about ongoing wealth management once they retire. The numbers, of course, are critical. We can't confidently recommend that people retire if they're not going to be financially stable or if the life they've envisioned isn't possible given their current projected cash flow. However, before we even talk about the financial possibility of retirement, we now dive into a much more personal conversation with our clients.

This qualitative side of retirement planning has often been overlooked in the financial-planning profession.

---

2 www.hzcapital.com.

I've been working in the business for a long time, and I can honestly say that only in the past two or three years have nonfinancial conversations about retirement readiness been openly discussed among my colleagues in the industry.

Too often, pre-retirees work for 30-plus years building a career, sometimes in a single industry, then walk away without looking back when they retire. What they don't realize is that they've spent more than three decades building much more than a career. They've been:

- Organizing a routine that's comfortable and familiar

- Honing skills and capabilities

- Forming lifelong relationships with close friends

- Building a social network for events and after-work connection

- Creating a purpose-driven life

The day that they wake up as a retiree is often the day that they walk away from many of those fundamentals. In other words, their career has played a major role in creating their identity. In hindsight, this played a large role in my mom's depression and, ultimately, contributed to her passing away.

This is why, in my own life *and* my business, I've

started exploring the nonfinancial side of retirement. When working with clients, we ask a lot of uncomfortable questions that they may not have previously considered. For example:

- What skills do you possess?

- What do you love about your career?

- How are you going to find that same joy, or use those skills, when you retire?

- How can you live a life of purpose in retirement?

- What are your plans as a retiree? How do you plan to spend an average Tuesday?

In my own life, I often reread the book *Halftime: Moving from Success to Significance* by Bob P. Buford. Some of the topics he covers about viewing retirement as the "halftime" in your own life truly resonate with me. The primary point Buford makes is that life is, essentially, divided into two halves. Retirement shouldn't be a finish line. Instead, it should just be another chapter in your life that you approach with the same dedication and planning you did your career. However, before you can pursue the second half of your life, you need to take a break. Just as there's a halftime show at the Super Bowl, retirees need their own halftime before pursuing whatever is next for them in their path to fulfillment.

Buford recommends taking time to fully decompress. That allows you, he says, to make space for the critical thinking and inspiration required to find the right next steps for you personally.

We encourage all of our clients to take and embrace this halftime. Too often, when retirees jump into the "next thing" the second they leave their careers behind, they find themselves continuing a pattern of burnout. It's easy to remain unfulfilled when you don't give yourself the breathing room you need to stop, enjoy your day-to-day, and create a clear break between the first and second halves of your life.

The truth is, you've worked hard for your retirement. You deserve to enjoy it. Someday, when I retire, I want to love every minute of it. You have every right to rest, relax, travel, and check items off your bucket list. But when the initial excitement of retirement wears off, you also deserve to enjoy a purpose-filled life every day.

You owe it to yourself to continue asking questions about whether you're fulfilled and whether you feel good as a retiree. Be open to the realization that goalposts can move. You may feel less fulfilled in Year 5 of your retirement than you did in Year 1, and that's okay. You're allowed to pivot and explore new lifestyle options for yourself.

The following chapters will go over how to build your unique, purpose-based retirement plan. We'll cover activities, ways to match your skills and interests to a retirement lifestyle, and how to balance your lifestyle goals with your budget. Most importantly, we'll go over how to have ongoing conversations about retirement with yourself, your spouse or partner, and with your loved ones *before* you retire.

I know that my mom would be proud if she knew her story could positively impact others. She was a giving person, and part of her legacy will be helping other retirees navigate the retirement transition and find joy in this new phase of their lives.

Chapter 3

UNDERSTANDING RETIREMENT AND DEPRESSION

lthough my mom's story isn't the norm for most retirees, the truth is that a retired adult is almost twice as likely to experience depression symptoms than a pre-retiree. Approximately 25 percent of adults age 65 or older deal with mental health issues. Even more concerning are the suicide rates for retired men, which hits a peak at age 75 or older according to the Centers for Disease Control.

Even if you don't face depression, the retirement blues are an all-too-common experience among new retirees. The truth is that many Americans view retirement as the ultimate goal. It's a finish line that they're excited to cross. This perception makes sense if you think about it.

Retirement in the media and in most advertising targeted toward pre-retirees depicts retirement as a golden paradise. Images of golfing in Florida, snorkeling in Hawaii, taking dance classes on Tuesday afternoons, and spending time with grandkids, family, and friends all come to mind.

However, often when you wake up on Day 1 of retirement, you're stuck staring at your four surrounding walls and wondering: *What am I going to do today?*

Obviously, you can't golf in Florida or snorkel in Hawaii every day of the week! It can feel overwhelming to transition from a full-time career where you're filled with purpose and a daily structure or routine to several decades' worth of nothing but time. Remember, you could be retired for 20–30 years—or more.

As a result, some retirees start to show the same psychological signs as someone who is severely overworked—even if they're watching daytime television every day of the week. Ideally, you'll be able to plan to sidestep these mental health roadblocks. However, in order to start building a retirement plan that works for you, you need to know the obstacles you could potentially face. Let's talk about a few of the issues that you should keep an eye out for.

Career Burnout

The main problem I see pre-retirees face as they get close to retirement is career burnout. In these cases, it seems like retirement would be the solution they're desperately seeking. After decades in their career, pre-retirees are tired of working. They're ready to transition to a stress-free life, not having to worry about keeping up with workplace politics or the demands of their job. This was certainly the case with my mom. She was so ready to retire that everyone was surprised when she suddenly started having second thoughts, followed by feelings of depression when she finally stopped working.

My dad, in particular, noticed the startling difference in her view of retirement before and after she retired. He remembered how desperate she was to leave the burdens of her full-time job as a hospice coordinator behind. There was a push in her industry to digitize, and she was sick of the pressure and unhappy with the future direction of her field.

Many people face similar feelings in the run-up to retirement. As the workplace environment shifts and changes, they may feel frustrated that things aren't the way they used to be, or they may just be overworked, overtired, and burned out. They become so focused on retirement as the solution to the frustrations they're feeling that they put blinders on.

In my mom's case, she was so frustrated with the sudden red tape and digital work she had to complete for her work that she wanted to retire as soon as possible. She knew she would miss the personal relationships she'd developed with hospice patients and their families one-on-one.

However, she didn't think about the fact that those connections and sense of purpose she had had in her job wouldn't reappear after retirement. She was so focused on getting out of the rat race that she never thought about how she'd find the purpose she was looking for once her career was over.

Lack of Structure

When you're working full time, your days have a specific structure to them. Even if your work schedule is flexible, and even if you're largely responsible for how you spend your work time, you undoubtedly have a routine. Your time at the office (or at home, if you work remotely) provides a template for your week. Your hours are set and accounted for, including the specific social interactions that provide entertainment and connection.

You may also have a routine that you've developed with your spouse or other family members as a result of how your work schedule structures your week. For example, weekends may be the time to spend with your family and friends. Weeknights might be for certain scheduled activities or pursuing your hobbies. Retirement can upend these expectations.

I've heard the wife of one retiree explain it like this: "I married you for better or worse but not for lunch!" She was accustomed to being home during the day, running errands and taking care of her own projects while her husband was at work during his 30- year career. All of a sudden, he wanted to be part of her day. It turned out that they had quite different visions for what their retired routine would look like. It was something they had never talked about before her husband's retirement, yet it created a new set of challenges they needed to overcome.

Loss of Purpose

Even if you're eager to retire and don't equate your self-worth to the success you've achieved in your career, retiring can create a jarring loss of purpose. Often we spend more time working than we do with our families or pursuing our other hobbies and passions in life. There are 168 hours in a week, and assuming you spend 50–60 of those hours sleeping, you have a little over 100 hours a week to occupy any way you choose. As a pre-retiree, 40–60 of those hours are spent working and growing your career.

Your job offers structure to your day and your life, but the sheer amount of time you spend pursuing goals, completing projects, and interacting with coworkers and clients is astounding. When you retire, you go from spending 50–60 percent of your available time working to having that time free to fill as you please.

Retiring takes those pursuits and sense of purpose and accomplishment away from you. Beyond that, you may also feel a loss of self. Our social culture strongly identifies who you are with what you do. When you take what you do out of the picture, it's easy to lose confidence in your identity and your capabilities as an individual.

This transition can be incredibly challenging, and if you're unable to translate the unique abilities you possess to how you spend your life as a retiree, you may be in for an emotional upheaval. If you don't have a plan for how to live a purpose-filled life after you retire, it becomes easy to slide into a case of the retirement blues or, as in the case of my mom, full-blown depression.

Lack of Planning

As they put aside the structure and sense of purpose a career offers, many retirees struggle to fill their hours. At first, filling 40–60 newly available hours may seem like a golden opportunity to pursue the hobbies and activities once reserved for weeknights, weekends, and holidays. However, many retirees quickly realize that the things they enjoy simply aren't time-consuming enough to complete their days. You can only read, paint, or golf so much before you tire or lose interest.

Deciding ahead of time how you want to fill an average Tuesday can dramatically reduce the pressure you feel once you enter retirement. This might mean creating a new structure or routine, signing up for a part-time job or volunteer position, intensifying your existing hobbies, or trying new ones.

Lack of Community

Many adults enjoy "circles" of community in different areas of their lives. For example, you may have a faith-based circle, a group of family and friends, or a close-knit group of coworkers and colleagues. It's easy to think that, after you retire, you'll just increase the amount of time you spend with the folks in these circles outside of work. However, 40–60 hours each week is a lot of time to fill, and it can be tough to fully replace a lost sense of connection.

Family, for example, may be less inclined than you imagined to help occupy your time. Your kids may have full-time careers of their own, and grandkids are in school for the majority of the day. Some of your friends may already be retired and happy to share time, but many other friends may still be making the retirement transition. A faith-based community might be available on Sundays and at some weekday events but not full time.

Before retiring, it's critical to think about what your community will look like. The phrase "no man is an island" rings especially true for retirees. Human beings are made to connect with other people.

Luckily, finding connections these days can be easier

than ever with the prevalence of digital options and the ability to search your local community for groups and events. Nevertheless, if you don't have a game plan in place, you're likely to suffer a feeling of isolation, anxiety, and, perhaps, depression.

Financial Stress

Even if you have confirmed with a financial advisor (as my mom had) that you're monetarily prepared to retire, financial stress may still be a stumbling block you face. It can be jarring to go from saving and seeing the account balance in your portfolio go up to watching the amount dwindle as you pull funds from your retirement savings accounts to fund your lifestyle. Many retirees are unsettled by this shift.

It's also challenging to know exactly how to create an income from your retirement savings that will last a lifetime. Individuals working with an advisor have an advantage, because they'll have a retirement-income plan set up and an accountability partner to help them adjust as needed over time and as circumstances change. However, the majority of retirees manage their retirement-income strategy on their own and may be unsure of the best way to structure withdrawals. Does this sound familiar? Here are some questions you may find daunting:

- When should I take Social Security?

- When do I need to start taking Required Minimum Distributions (RMDs) from my IRA?

- Will my pension cover most of my expenses?

- How should I elect to take my pension? Should I consider my spouse when deciding which election option to take?

- Which retirement account should I start drawing from first?

- What happens if I need more (or less) money than I'm withdrawing?

- What happens if we face a recession or bear market when I'm retired?

- How can I ensure that there's some of my wealth left over to give to my family?

- What if I don't have enough money coming in from my savings, Social Security, or my pension to live the retirement lifestyle I've always dreamed of?

- What if I get sick or require long-term care?

The truth is that there's a lot to consider when you're entering retirement, and these types of questions are enough to cause any retiree to feel overwhelmed and off-kilter. Having a financial strategy in place helps, but, of course, your finances and lifestyle are likely to shift over the course of your retirement. It's critical to address the financial stress you may feel and create a system that works for you both now and in the future.

Although I'm obviously biased, I also believe that it's crucial to have a financial advisor you trust giving you guidance throughout the retirement journey. A trusted advisor is trained to give you advice on these questions and more! A good advisor will also keep you from making any big mistakes along the way and will counsel you against any irrational decisions you might be tempted to make.

• • •

Many of these stumbling blocks are common for retirees to face, but there's a way to overcome them. With some forward thinking you can turn them into stepping-stones toward the retirement you've always imagined!

In the chapters to come, I'm going to walk you through these key stumbling blocks, and suggest how you can plan to turn them into your very own retirement stepping-stones. We'll go over everything from identifying your values to building a financial plan for your dream retirement. Let's get started!

Chapter 4

STUMBLING BLOCKS/ STEPPING-STONES— AN OVERVIEW

In this chapter, I'll preview the key stumbling blocks you could face as a new retiree and the stepping-stones that can lead to your retirement success. Each of the following chapters will treat the pair in depth.

1. Loss of Purpose/Identify Your Values

When your career provides you with a sense of purpose and accomplishment, it's critical to determine why. Your answer won't be the same as your spouse's or your coworkers'. That's because we each find purpose and accomplishment in our lives for different reasons that are largely dependent on our unique set of values.

Everyone has a set of values that steers their decision-making—the choices they make in their career, relationships, and so much more. One key to building your ideal retirement is to understand your personal values and how they impact your life. Once you've determined what your values are, you can make decisions about how you spend your resources—both time and money—during retirement, and rest assured that you'll find fulfillment even if you aren't receiving a sense of purpose from your career.

2. A Loss of Self and Engagement/ Define Your Dreams

Another stumbling block many new retirees face is a loss of self and the resulting inability to engage with the world around them. Knowing your values will help you feel more confident in who you are and what matters to you. However, in order to truly connect with yourself and your life during this new season of life, you need to define your dream retirement.

It's often said that you can't hit a target you can't see. If you've put on the "retirement blinders" that come with career burnout, you may not have thought of what your dream retirement entails. Vague visions of sunshine-filled days with grandkids at the park or extended beach vacations might be in the back of your mind. But have you ever asked what will truly make you happy in retirement?

During this step, I'll help you define your dream retirement, including how to imagine an alternate retirement that's rarely advertised in the mainstream media. We'll cover everything from vacations and relocation to deciding whether you'd prefer full-time retirement or an encore career. You have many options available, and it's important to know what your "ideal" looks like before your last day of work.

3. Feeling Underprepared for Retirement/ Align Your Values

The last thing you want is to wake up on the Monday after you retire only to feel overwhelmed by the sheer amount of empty time you have on your hands. My mom absolutely went through this. She often talked about how, after retiring, the initial excitement wore off and anxiety immediately took its place. Although part of this was about how she viewed her self-worth as a health care provider, another part of it arose from the fact that she didn't have a plan for how to fill her time.

This retirement stepping-stone is all about aligning your day-to-day routine as a retiree with your values to create a fulfilling structure for your new life. Retirement is an exciting new chapter, but many retirees find themselves stressed out, overwhelmed, or just plain bored. Knowing that you have predetermined activities or an idea of your new routine going into retirement can alleviate a lot of stress.

4. Loss of Connection/Planning to Connect

Losing 40–60 hours a week of constant connection and interaction can be overwhelming and, frankly, depressing. As I've noted, we are built for human connection. Having long-lasting relationships and ongoing interaction is what makes life worth living (even if you're an introvert!). You can take steps before you retire to maintain relationships and start new ones.

In this retirement stepping-stone, we'll go over how you can have conversations with the key people in your life *before* you retire to lay the groundwork for fulfilling relationships later.

These conversations can also help you gain a deeper understanding of what your friends and family expect from your relationship during this new season of your life. Communication is key to maintaining relationships, and the sooner you start talking to the people who matter most to you, the sooner you can count on those relationships throughout retirement.

5. Lifestyle Changes/Taking Actionable Steps Beforehand

Many retirees are jarred by their massive lifestyle transition. Taking actionable steps before retirement to adjust your lifestyle and expectations will help you ease into a new retirement lifestyle.

You might consider:

- Downsizing if necessary
- Relocating, if that's part of your retirement plan
- "Test driving" any dramatic lifestyle changes you're considering (like becoming a snowbird during the winter)

The last thing you want is to retire to a completely new life. Even though that may sound appealing, it could result in a deep sense of unrest and unhappiness. Humans thrive with consistency and clear expectations. Easing into your retirement lifestyle as a pre-retiree or early in retirement can help you mitigate the culture shock that comes with retirement.

6. Are You Financially Ready?/Building an Airtight Budget

As a financial advisor, I can't deny that knowing the financial ins and outs of your retirement plan is key to finding peace and fulfillment in retirement. Once you've outlined your values, your dream retirement, and a backup lifestyle plan, it's time to pull together a retirement financial plan with a financial planner.

Together, we'll walk through how to take the technical elements of your finances and connect them to the values-based lifestyle you're working hard to build. In this retirement stepping-stone, we'll talk about projecting your retirement cash-flow needs, how to build an income strategy, and ways you can stress test your financial plan for a worst-case scenario.

7. Financial Anxiety/Understanding Dollars and Cents

Not sure where your retirement income is coming from? You're not alone. Deciphering the many types of accounts and sources of income during retirement can be exhausting. To turn this stumbling block into a stepping-stone, we will review each source of retirement income and go over how to create an income plan that works for you.

8. Health Care Questions/ Exploring Your Options

Understanding insurance after retirement can feel like navigating a minefield of potentially costly mistakes. Your health is the foundation of everything else in your life. Without it, you won't be able to enjoy the retirement you've worked so hard to build. This is why it's so important to prioritize your health through your retirement budget. By setting funds aside to ensure your needs are met, you're setting up a lifestyle that will work for you regardless of any health problems you may face.

9. It's Not What It's Cracked Up to Be/ Have a Backup Plan

Some retirees start retirement with no signs of the retirement blues. They thrive on tackling home renovation projects and going fishing every day. This is, after all, the retirement they dreamed about—right?

Unfortunately, these same people often experience a delayed sense of purposelessness. They burn out on retirement because they do too much too soon. They're knocking off bucket-list items like traveling, buying a boat, becoming a snowbird, and spending copious amounts of time with family and friends.

Then, a few years into retirement, they realize this lifestyle may not be sustainable. It may be financially challenging, or they slowly start to realize that constantly focusing on the next adventure isn't emotionally fulfilling.

This is where having a Plan B can be helpful. Not everyone wants to be retired full time for the rest of their lives. In fact, my sister and I have often wondered if my mom would still be with us if she'd pursued a Plan B of her own.

During this retirement stepping-stone, we'll go over your options—from full-time retirement or volunteer work to working part time or pursuing further education. We'll go over how to build a backup plan and how to stress test your retirement lifestyle.

10. Want to Make an Impact/ Create Your Legacy

In the final retirement stepping-stone, we'll talk about making an impact. Many retirees worry that they won't leave a legacy or that their life's impact diminishes as they age. You can offset this fear by having an estate plan that prioritizes leaving a legacy as you enter retirement. I'll walk you through how to create an estate plan that's streamlined and that prioritizes the people and causes you're most passionate about. We'll also cover starting estate-planning conversations with your loved ones.

• • •

I encourage you to visit my website www.tonyhixon.com and download the *Retirement Stepping Stones Workbook*, available for free. It serves as a companion piece to this book, and it will elevate your experience and set you on a trajectory of retirement preparedness.

Let's look at each of these stumbling blocks in depth, and discover together how to turn them into retirement stepping-stones.

Chapter 5

IDENTIFY YOUR VALUES

Stumbling Block #1: Loss of Purpose

As we've noted, many retirees feel an unexpected loss of purpose when they enter retirement. Obviously, as with my mom, some retirees experience this in a much deeper and more harmful way than others. We should recognize that we're often encouraged to find self-value and purpose in our careers. If you really think about it, you've been told since you were 17 or 18 years old that the job you get, the degree you obtain, and the career you build defines who you are.

Unfortunately, this type of thinking can prevent pre-retirees from taking the time to truly identify their core values. Instead, they focus on general, workplace-related values and let those define their lives. There's nothing wrong with this. In fact, most pre-retirees prioritize workplace-related values not because they're superficial or even workaholics; they're just burned out. Think about it. For the past several *decades*, you've undoubtedly spent a great deal of effort building and growing your career.

Now, just before retirement, you're enjoying the fruits of your labor. Your career has grown, you're making more money, and you're likely operating at a more senior level or position in your line of work. However, higher positions come with more responsibilities and fewer opportunities to spend your time in ways that you want. Your schedule may be so full that you haven't had time to think about how you want to spend retirement. Your mental capacity is already taken up with work. The only next step you can think about is reaching the retirement milestone. Anything after that seems hazy.

If this sounds like you, don't worry! You still have plenty of time to remedy the situation.

Retirement Stepping-Stone #1: Identify Your Values

There are several ways you can identify your values and then use those values to find purpose and meaning during retirement. Remember, this type of introspection is going to be time consuming. I recommend you take a day or an afternoon off from work and out of your normal routine.

Table your to-do list, and find the time and space to do some reflection.

Many people haven't examined their values recently, if ever. Don't be intimidated by the process. Yes, sitting alone with your thoughts and thinking about your values can feel uncomfortable—especially if you're not used to self-reflection! If you start to feel that discomfort increasing, take a break. Remind yourself that, as unusual or uncomfortable as this exercise might be, it's going to help you live a fulfilling and happy retirement—something that we're all striving toward.

I recommend checking out the Barrett Values Centre, which provides both personal values assessments, as well as exercises for larger organizations. The tools and workshops offered by the Barrett Values Centre are based on the research done by Richard Barrett, whose model focuses on seven key areas of human motivation. The Barrett Values Centre offers a free Personal Values Assessment[3] to help you determine what you hold dear. The survey is relatively succinct. You are offered a list of possible values and are asked to pick a maximum of 10. Following the assessment, a packet detailing your top 10 selected values and exercises that guide your future self-development and exploration are sent to your email address.

---

3 "Personal Values Assessment: Understanding Your Values," Barrett Values Centre, accessed February 6, 2021, https://www.valuescentre.com/tools-assessments/pva.

Of course, you can always identify your values by working through several steps on your own.

Step One: Define What "Values" Are

Before diving into these values-defining exercises, it can help to simply focus on *what values are.*

A value can be defined as your principles or what you judge to be important in life. The truth is that values can be derived from many different motivating factors. Some may come from a need to meet basic survival requirements. Others may stem from selfless service or a desire to make a difference in the world.

Typically, your values are what guide your decisions, inform your actions, and dictate how you spend your time and energy. Often, when you're close to retirement and experiencing some burnout, what you are involved in may not be aligned with what you truly value.

For example, if you're working 60–80-hour weeks in a demanding, manager-level position at your company, you may not have the emotional or mental space after hours or on weekends to volunteer or invest in your relationships with friends and family. When you're in survival mode, your values are harder to act on. In these cases, it can help to think back to early in your career when you were bright-eyed and ready to take on the world.

Step Two: Think Back to Your Past Values

The first, and possibly most important, factor to recognize is that your values are fluid. When you are entering retirement, your values are likely dramatically different than what they were when you were a newly minted college graduate or were just entering the workforce. Remembering those values can help you determine whether they've changed with time and what your values are during this season of your life. For example, your early career values may have been:

- Family: Providing for your young family and spending time with your kids.

- Self-Improvement: Continuing your education.

- Faith: Attending gatherings.

- Loyalty: Staying true to your employer and your colleagues in workplace interactions.

- Ambition: Being driven to continually challenge yourself in work and in life, looking for opportunities to move up and gain responsibility.

These are just a few of the possibilities. Take a moment to think back to when you first started your career, and jot down a few of the values that guided your decisions then and the way you spent your time.

Step Three: Think Through Your
Current Values and Purpose

How do you currently spend your time? What do you value most? These questions are tough to tackle. You can start by thinking about how you find purpose in your daily life. Perhaps it's when you achieve your goals at work. Or maybe it's when you connect with your loved ones at a yearly family reunion.

If these ideas are coming to mind easily, great! Jot them down as they occur to you. Then, distill those purpose-driven activities you enjoy into values. Let's look at a few examples:

If you find purpose when you achieve your goals at work, you might value challenge, responsibility, or accomplishment.

If you find purpose when someone notices that you've achieved your goals at work, you might value the respect of others.

If you find purpose in connecting with your loved ones, you might value family, friends, and relationships.

Struggling to clearly define your values? Don't worry— you're not alone! It can help to look at a list of values and think about those that most closely connect to the activities and events that give you a feeling of purpose or joy. The following list can help you get started:

Abundance	Diversity	Making an Impact
Acceptance	Empathy	Personal Development
Achievement	Family	Security
Adventure	Friendships	Relationships
Balance	Generosity	Responsibility
Calm	Happiness	Simplicity
Challenge	Health	Teamwork
Community	Honesty	Understanding
Compassion	Leadership	Wealth
Creativity	Learning	Well-Being

This is just a short list to get the ball rolling! There are many resources available that offer a much longer list of values. If you search for "values list" on the internet you can find lists with 50–100 values for you to consider.

Still struggling to define your values? Sometimes we don't see ourselves as clearly as others do. This is where talking to a spouse, partner, family member, or trusted mentor can really help. Sit down with someone you love and whose opinion you respect and have an honest conversation about your values. They may be better able to see your actions and accomplishments honestly and help you clarify what you value most and how you find purpose.

Step Four: Consider Your Unique Ability®[4]

Everyone has a unique ability. (Some people might even have several!) These strengths often inform what you value most in life, and pursuing them can bring you an immense sense of purpose and well-being. But what is a unique ability? And how can you find it?

The concept of a Unique Ability®[5] comes from Dan Sullivan, founder of The Strategic Coach. I originally found Dan's work years ago through his coaching program for entrepreneurs. At the time, I was relatively new to entrepreneurship. I knew that my business partner, Adam, and I wanted to create a financial-planning company that truly made an impact in the lives of others. Through our previous work as accountants at different firms, we had heard the stories of countless people who were overconfident in developing their business plans on their own, only to realize (often too late) that they had made colossal errors in estimating how far their wealth would take them. Worse still, we heard about financial

---

4 Unique Ability® is a trademarked name from Strategic Coach®, a Dan Sullivan company, https://uniqueability.com/.
5 "What Is Unique Ability®, UniqueAbility.com, accessed February 6, 2021, https://uniqueability.com/.

"advisors" who led their clients astray time and again with faulty advice or investment ideas that cost people an arm and a leg in management fees over the course of their retirement.

When Adam and I first went into business together, we knew we wanted to turn the tides and offer a holistic financial-planning firm that helped people adequately plan for their financial future. One of the most common financial goals people have is to retire. So, like many other financial advisors, we chose retirement planning as our specialty. It was where we felt we could make the most impact. Our clients were facing one of the biggest financial turning points of their lives, and we were ready to help.

However, despite having a purpose-driven business and a like-minded business partner, I still felt a deeper pull to gain an understanding of who I was as a business owner and as a person. I wanted to know how I could move the needle in my business, serve our clients in a deeper way, and connect with people in my life more meaningfully. In other words, I had hit the point that many people hit well before retirement: I wanted to figure out my life's purpose before it was too late.

Through the Strategic Coach program, I was able to uncover my purpose, set some big goals for myself and my business, and create a concrete action plan to help me achieve them. During this program, I also explored my own Unique Ability®. According to Dan Sullivan's program, your Unique Ability® is what drives you. For example, my Unique Ability® Statement is: providing steady, disciplined leadership; delivering consistent, positive results; and nurturing deep, authentic relationships in order to continually drive progress forward to fulfill my unique purpose and inspire others to fulfill theirs.

The program walks you through eight Unique Ability® mind-sets:

1. Acknowledge unique talents.

2. Pursue greater self-awareness.

3. Be honest about self.

4. Be open to influence and growth.

5. Have passion-driven courage.

6. Value other people's unique talents.

7. Be responsible for designing your own life.

8. Seek a better, more meaningful life.

Each mind-set offers a range of opportunities for growth and reflection. For example, you may acknowledge that you have some unique talents but aren't sure how to take advantage of those strengths in life. Alternatively, you may be acutely aware of your strengths and feel confident about what, exactly, drives you toward success.

Understanding my own Unique Ability® changed how I lived my life and how I plan for the future. I believe that many pre-retirees have never considered what their ability might be and how it impacts their ability to find success and fulfillment in life's next chapter.

The good news is that you don't have to go through the Strategic Coach program, or even be an entrepreneur, to determine your own Unique Ability®. Dan Sullivan's book, *Unique Ability® 2.0: Discovery*, is readily available.[6] Through his website, Sullivan also provides a number of free resources to help you kick off your self-exploration, including blog posts, a self-assessment scorecard that identifies areas for personal development, a book club, and a quick guide for people who want an overview.

After going through the program myself, I became interested in helping others find their own. I'm convinced that we are each created for a purpose. We are all unique in our own way; even identical twins have different fingerprints! It's also my belief that everyone is blessed with a unique ability. You've likely always had it, ever since you were a small child. However, figuring out what your unique ability is can be even harder than defining your values! It's rare that we have the ability to look inward and uncover the gifts we're blessed with. The process may

6 *Unique Ability® 2.0: Discovery*, Unique Ability®, accessed February 6, 2021, https://uniqueability.com/the-book/.

be uncomfortable and can even feel self-aggrandizing. Nobody likes to feel full of themselves!

This is another great time to engage a friend in conversation. Choose those who know you best, and have them tell you how they view you. After speaking with a handful of people, it's usually pretty easy to find a common thread. For example, let's look at my mom's unique ability.

Anyone who knew my mother knew that her unique ability was, beyond a shadow of a doubt, her ability to care for others. She was easily one of the most giving people I knew. My sister says, "She was gifted in a really cool way. She was a prayer warrior and an encourager."

My mom's unique ability was to lift others up. This even showed up in her career choice. Hospice care isn't for the faint of heart. Caring for the sick and dying and comforting their families is exhausting, heart-wrenching work. Yet my mom loved it and was endlessly passionate about her patients. Even toward the end of her career, the burnout she experienced was never because she was tired of the work itself. She was tired of the red tape and the office politics that made it harder for her to care for others.

My mom chose a career as an RN and hospice-care worker, but her gift showed up in other ways, too. She volunteered with her church, spent time with her friends, and constantly acted as a cheerleader for her family. If she had been able to take a closer look inside herself to see her own unique gift, she could have nurtured her abilities throughout retirement.

Lynette adds, "There were other avenues for her to pursue. From essential oils to holistic health, she could have morphed [her love of care for others] into something. She just felt too scared or afraid to do something with it."

Your goal should be to take an unflinching look at what gives you a sense of purpose, what you value, and your unique gift to determine how you can bring value into the world beyond your last day at the office.

Step Five: Determine Whether Your Values Need to Shift

More often than not, when you experience burnout in the years leading up to retirement, you're living in survival mode. You aren't necessarily being intentional with your time and energy—and that's okay. We all move through seasons of life where we're simply trying to keep our head above water.

Instead of focusing on the fact that you aren't living in a way that makes you happy, focus instead on what values need to shift to experience a fulfilling retirement. For example, if one of your unique abilities is the ability to listen and support others, you might find that while you're at work you're spending time listening to and supporting your subordinates and colleagues. This is noble work

RETIREMENT STEPPING STONES

and can be required to keep the office running smoothly! However, maybe you want to connect this unique ability to your core value of faith during retirement. This could show up as:

- Mentoring teens at your church or place of worship

- Volunteering to speak with family members whose loved ones are in hospice care

- Spending more time having heartfelt conversations with your faith-based study group about their lives

The questions you have to ask yourself are:
What is it that I'm going to do every day?
What skills have I acquired that I can utilize to help others?
How will society need me?
It's also important to note that not everyone will value structure, or the security of having a plan for how to spend retirement. In fact, many people may value the opposite—freedom from routine. I know several people, clients included, who have dreaded the idea of falling into yet another ho-hum routine in retirement. They want the excitement that comes with flexibility, adventure, and getting to make decisions about their lifestyle without the constraints of a career holding them back. If this sounds familiar to you, know that

having a plan for your retirement doesn't have to mean you're locked in. The truth is that your retirement is just that—yours. You get to create both a financial and a lifestyle plan that gives you the flexibility you need to remain open to opportunities, and to be able to pivot at a moment's notice.

Let's look at an example of how remaining flexible, or embracing spontaneity in life, might look. During your career, you may have experienced a lot of rapid upward movement. Your willingness to pursue new opportunities led you to take promotions, relocate for exciting new job prospects, and complete training that gave you an expanded knowledge of your field. In retirement, you may be tempted to think that what drove you all along was the desire to advance in your career. While this may be partially true, you might feel incredibly disappointed if you continue to pursue growth aggressively in retirement through an encore career or another path that puts you in a monotonous routine. Instead, you could incorporate your spontaneous personality by:

- Building enough "buffer" in your financial plan to successfully allow for lifestyle changes during retirement should you choose to pursue them.

- Opening yourself up to new opportunities, like living abroad for a time, traveling via motorhome for a year, or exploring continuing education.

- Reducing the number of things in your life that
  tie you down. This could mean downsizing your
  home or limiting yourself and your spouse to a
  single vehicle.

Regardless of what your values are, you can fulfill
your purpose beyond your career. If you're not happy
with how you've been spending your time lately, or you
feel it doesn't align with your values or your unique gift,
that's okay. Take this time to think about how you can
shift your focus in this new chapter of your life. Retirement isn't the shutting of a door—it's the start of a new
and exciting adventure where *you* get to make the rules.
That's an exciting prospect to look forward to.

Chapter 6

DEFINING YOUR DREAM RETIREMENT

Stumbling Block #2: Feeling a Void after Retirement

Now it's time to map out exactly what your dream retirement looks like. People in their 50s and 60s too often start thinking about retirement as the natural next step in their lives without planning ahead. They're usually burned out after decades of working in the same industry, often with the same people. They look around and see their friends retiring and are ready to take the leap themselves, often thinking of retirement as a finish line of sorts.

As someone who regularly trains for triathlons, I understand this mindset. There's something energizing in training for a big race every year. The training schedule that helps me structure my days, the "me" time that comes with planning, and the excitement I feel when I hit training milestones as race day gets closer—all of these things are part of the journey that gets me to the finish line.

However, it's equally important to plan for what comes *after* a triathlon. Rest, recovery, and rehabilitation after a physically taxing event are critical. I've been racing in triathlons for years, so I know that the days, weeks, and months after a race are important for my mental and physical health. This isn't always true for others. Many new racers skip postrace planning. That's understandable. Triathlons are no small accomplishment. When you finish, all you want to do is be *done*.

I find that pre-retirees often experience similar emotions. Think of your career as training for that finish-line moment. The years leading up to retirement when you're checking your savings and ensuring you'll be financially comfortable are the race. You're playing catch-up, streamlining your strategy, and working to end your career on a high note.

Then your last day of work rolls around. This is the moment you've been waiting for your entire career. You enjoy the celebratory cake, thank your coworkers for the balloons and the party, then you go home.

Now what?

Many retirees have envisioned spending time on their boat, hanging out with their grandkids, sleeping in, or gardening. They may have grand ideas about international travel or spending their winters in sunny Arizona.

Still, when they wake up to their first full day as retirees, there's often a void awaiting them. They were so desperate to just make it to retirement and leave their careers behind that they didn't think about what comes after. Day-to-day retirement life isn't something they had planned for, and it's certainly not as thrilling as the life of expensive travel, dinners out, and hours spent making family memories.

The truth is that planning for reality doesn't seem very exciting, so people skip it. The same is true for triathlon racers. The event itself is exciting. Crossing the finish line and taking a picture pumping your fist victoriously is exhilarating! That's the moment you've planned for. The reality of sore muscles, rehabilitation training, and required rest are notably less compelling.

In fact, it's common for race participants to experience a kind of slump after completing a triathlon. The moment you've worked for is over, and that can be an emotional letdown. I find that many retirees experience this same slump in the time after they stop working. This slump should last only a brief period of time. However, in cases like my mom's, a slump can deepen into a harmful depression. Of course, not every slump spirals out of control. Let's look at a more common example.

Slumping Steve

Slumping Steve retired with no expectations of continuing work. In fact, all he had on his retirement agenda was to rest, spend time with loved ones, and live life in the moment. Of course, that's often easier said than done—especially when you come from a fast-paced work environment.

Steve had been a business owner prior to retirement. He was always on the go and thrived in the world of entrepreneurship. For Steve, daily life was defined by a lack of routine. He was always tackling his next big idea, balancing life and client work, and managing his employees. When he sold his business, he had nothing but high hopes for the early stages of retirement. He assumed that transitioning into a world with the same flexibility as entrepreneurship, without all of the pressure of business ownership, would be a welcome change of pace. Steve viewed retirement as his next big idea—and he was up for the adventure.

Steve retired in late August, and the first few months of retirement went well. He checked all the items off of his list and relished waking up each day with a blank slate. For once in his life, Steve could spend his time however he wanted without any stressful demands. Through December of that year, life couldn't have been more ideal.

- Steve traveled to his bucket-list location of Australia with his wife.

- He spent extended and focused time with his kids and grandchildren.

- He tried new restaurants with family and friends.

- He took an art class at his local community college.

- He enjoyed having his first holiday season without the pressures of his business weighing him down.

- He made plans with his wife to start renovating their house to include a covered porch and an expanded vegetable garden in the spring.

Everyone Steve spoke with agreed that he was doing retirement "the right way." On paper, that looked to be true. He was, after all, having the time of his life.

Then, on January 1, reality hit Steve. Usually, he'd be planning for his annual team retreat. He'd be outlining company goals, running reports, and analyzing any weak points in his business. And he missed all of that. Steve had gotten so caught up in the glamour of retirement, he forgot something crucial about himself: As stressful as entrepreneurship was, he really, *really* liked it.

Steve lived for the strategy, planning, and drive that being a business owner required. Even though he ran into tense moments, where it felt like the stakes were high and big decisions had to be made, he loved getting to problem solve his way out of each tough situation he had faced over the years. Now, it suddenly felt like all of that was gone. He felt a little lost, unsure of what came next. After all, how many vacations to Australia or new art classes could he possibly take?

If Steve had taken the time to think through what

he wanted out of this next chapter beyond simply not owning his business anymore, he might have discovered that his dream retirement actually included a lot of elements of business ownership. He had focused too much on his big retirement checklist and not enough on the reality of his daily life. To resolve this issue, Steve decided to brainstorm ideas for how to spend his time week to week. These included looking into part-time consulting for other entrepreneurs and small businesses to help him stay connected to the elements of being a business owner that he used to love. Let's look at how you can avoid being like Slumping Steve and plan for your dream retirement ahead of time.

Retirement Stepping-Stone #2: Plan for Your Dream Retirement Ahead of Time

It's critical to plan ahead and build your dream retirement from the ground up. Let's talk about a few actionable steps you can take.

Be Honest with Yourself

The hard truth is that most people overhype retirement. When they think of life as a retiree, they think of every day as a big (often costly) adventure. When I speak with clients, they often mention:

- Making large purchases, like a boat, RV, or a new vehicle

- Relocating to a newer home in a different area

- Remodeling their existing home

- Traveling frequently

- Spending nearly all of their time with family

- Eating out or trying new restaurants

- Practicing an existing hobby like golf

- Picking up a new hobby like biking, boating, or painting

All of these desires are elements of a dream retirement. However, if they're all you picture when you retire, you may be disappointed to find that you still don't have much to fill the 8–10 hours you used to spend at work on any given Tuesday.

Additionally, if you focus only on the bigger, bucket-list parts of retirement, you may find that your savings doesn't support that vision. Here's where it's important to get honest with yourself: Is your image of retirement over-blown? How can you plan for reality, while still building the retirement of your dreams?

Write It Out

It may be helpful to physically write down what you want out of retirement. Don't limit yourself during this exercise. Jot down all of the big (and small) things you'd like to do or accomplish. Once this is complete, you'll have a clearer picture of what you really want—even if not all of your goals are financially feasible.

Struggling to Brainstorm?

If you're struggling to go beyond the basics of your retirement vision, reviewing your previous life and career can help. Ask yourself these questions:

What about my career did I enjoy?

You've spent anywhere from 30 to 40 years building your career. There must have been some element of the work that you enjoyed in that time period. Whether you loved specific tasks or you liked working with people you cared about, identifying what you liked to do as part of your profession can reveal what you may like to do in retirement.

Here's an example: If you loved working with people, you may want to find a way to volunteer with a team of other retirees who are passionate about the same cause or causes you are.

What about my career did I not enjoy?

Of course, for every single feature of your career that you liked, you may have a complementary list of aspects you weren't as interested in. Consider what's on this list. When you retire, how can you ensure you avoid these tasks or the way they make you feel?

Here's another example: If you didn't like having uncomfortable social interactions or you chafed under your workplace hierarchy but liked doing a task you knew you would do well, consider incorporating DIY projects into your retirement plan. These can be small, like starting a flower garden. They can also be larger and more challenging, like renovating parts of your house on your own (assuming you have that skill set).

How do I spend my time when I can freely choose what I would like to do?

When you have no prior commitments, and you don't have a coworker, friend, or family member dictating your calendar, what do you gravitate toward? If you're currently overwhelmed by burnout, the answer may be sleep, watching television, or practicing another activity that helps you to mentally check out. If that's the case, think back to a season when you were fully recharged or close to it. How did you spend your time then?

The answer may be something simple, like reading, or

it may surprise you to realize how often you headed to the lake to fish when your schedule allowed. The way you spend your time when nobody else has expectations for your schedule can be very telling.

Another example: If your default activity is curling up with a good book, you might think about joining a weekly or monthly book club to stay social while you do something you enjoy.

What have I always wanted to do or try?

Have you always wanted to improve your tennis skills? Does the thought of learning to throw pottery make you smile? Retirement is the perfect time to pursue continued education and personal development. Just because your career is over doesn't mean that your life stops. You can continue to grow and improve.

Maybe you took an oil-painting course in high school and enjoyed it but never pursued it again. College, a career, and raising a family got in the way. Now is the time to enroll in an art course! Many local community colleges offer free or discounted programs for seniors or retirees.

Do I have a unique skill set that could benefit others?

My mom had a unique skill set. As a hospice-care worker, she was good at emotionally supporting others. She comforted people as they passed away, and she brought peace to their families. Caring for people who were in need was truly her calling. Think about your own life. What unique skill set either from your career or personal activities could benefit others?

Perhaps over the course of your career, you've developed the necessary skills for leading a team and encouraging the members. In retirement, you could use this ability and amplify it by leading a youth group or volunteering as a part-time coach or club leader at your local high school.

What am I passionate about?

What activities or causes drive you? You may be passionate about:

- Family
- Friends and relationships
- Faith
- Politics
- Community

Or any number of other things. Finding ways to pursue and support those passions in retirement can help you feel more fulfilled.

One more example: Perhaps you're passionate about politics and your local community. As a retiree, you might volunteer for a local board or nonprofit or run for office to get more involved in your city government.

What-If Scenarios

It's always wise to consider what parts of your dream retirement plan are most important to you. If your vision is too expensive, you may need to cut back on something in order for your finances to adequately support your lifestyle. However, these trade-offs will feel less overwhelming or upsetting if you know what your priorities are.

Have the courage to run through several what-if scenarios. These might include:

- Financial turbulence

- Medical emergencies

- The need for long-term health care

How would these scenarios impact your dream retirement? This is where combining your values with your dream retirement lifestyle can help you to adjust expectations and move forward with confidence.

Chapter 7

ALIGNING YOUR LIFESTYLE AND YOUR VALUES

Stumbling Block #3: Feeling Underprepared Emotionally and Financially for the Reality of Retirement

This is the point where you put your newly discovered values and your dream retirement lifestyle together to create concrete goals. It can be challenging for pre-retirees to prioritize their desires for retirement when it comes to creating a lifestyle plan. It sounds great to be able to vacation in Italy once a year, visit out-of-state family frequently, buy a boat, remodel your home, and eat out with friends a few times a week. However, these expenses can quickly add up. Depending on your retirement savings, you may or may not be able to sustain the lifestyle of your dreams over the full course of your retirement.

Keep in mind that many people are retired for between 10 to 30-plus years. In that time period, your medical situation may change, and your financial needs will undoubtedly shift for one reason or another. These fluctuating expenses can throw your ideal retirement off course, and it can be challenging to balance goals and expenses if you aren't sure what will have the biggest impact on your quality of life.

Moreover, many retirees enter this new chapter of their lives with grand notions. They're often excited about tackling all of the bucket-list items that they've spent years dreaming about but aren't overly realistic about fitting those expenses into an ongoing budget. They may have not financially planned for making those dreams a reality, and, what's worse, they may also have overblown ideas of what retirement will be. The result? They are often disappointed.

Retirement Stepping-Stone #3: Align Your Lifestyle and Budget with Your Values

This is where creating a values-based plan for your retirement lifestyle comes in handy.

When your retirement budget and your lifestyle plan are both in alignment with what you value most, you'll find:

- You're more satisfied with your daily life as a retiree.

- Even if you have to make budget adjustments, your normal lifestyle should still be emotionally fulfilling.

- You're less likely to make impulsive spending decisions that could derail your finances in retirement.

- Both you and your spouse or partner will more easily transition from your career to retirement because you genuinely look forward to this new chapter of your life.

I know that this isn't an exercise my mom did before retiring. She was so burned out from work that simply the idea of *not working* was enough for her. You may be feeling the same way right now. If you're exhausted and ready to just be retired, you might be tempted to skip making an intentional, values-based plan for the future. Admittedly, this strategy may work at first.

People who are desperate to retire are often initially relieved once they cross that finish line. In fact, they may even continue to be content for a while simply because they're not going to work every day. I've found this with some of my financial-planning clients. They experience an initial glow in retirement because it's a novel way of living for them. These clients feel that getting to wake up when they want, see family whenever they'd like, and have general flexibility in their schedule is more than enough. More often than not, however, this honeymoon period doesn't last.

These are usually the same clients who, when I initially ask them about their retirement lifestyle and their values, may shrug it off. Alternatively, they may have general answers that depict a hazy idea of how they'd like to spend their time after retirement. Obviously, I never try to push clients to have conversations they're not ready for or that they don't want to engage in. So if they're adamant that they're ready to retire, even without a lifestyle plan, I let it go.

Usually during our ongoing check-ins and later conversations is when I find out they're unhappy. Luckily, because my relationship with my clients extends beyond a one-time engagement in most cases, I can help them see when they're out of alignment with their values. Together, we can look at their financial plan and make adjustments that support a much happier, fulfilling lifestyle for themselves and their spouse.

Joe and Susan

My clients Joe and Susan retired in the last year or so. They were ecstatic and dove headfirst into their number-one retirement lifestyle dream: They bought a vacation home in Arizona.

Now you have to understand, winters here in Ohio are gray and cold. I completely understood why they wanted to become snowbirds and spend the colder months in a place with warm weather and sunny skies. We had already built into their financial plan the purchase of a small condo for the two of them in Arizona.

The setup seemed ideal. Their condo was in a nice neighborhood with a homeowners association (HOA) that took care of their property when they were gone. There was neighborhood security that would ensure that their home and possessions were safe when they were living back in Ohio. The condo was close to all of the places and amenities that they loved when they visited. On paper, it was the perfect scenario.

They jumped into this new way of living because it was the one thing they had always planned on for their retirement. Both Joe and Susan knew that they were ready to be done working; they thought that living the dream in Arizona would be more than enough to allow them a fulfilling life after retirement.

I met with them about six months after they had moved into their condo. The plan was for us to review their finances and to do a general check-in since they were relatively newly retired.

It didn't take long for me to find out they were unhappy in Arizona.

In fact, I'd say they were miserable. Although they had both looked forward to life in the Southwest, they found they spent more time in their condo than enjoying the golf course, restaurants, or other hangouts they had fallen in love with on vacation. Both of them had assumed that every day would be as relaxing and exciting as during their previous trips. Instead, they felt stuck and frustrated.

Instead of reacting to their news with a quick decision to call Arizona quits and head home to Ohio, I took a moment to pause with them.

"Joe, Susan, let's talk about your values," I said.

They were both a little bit thrown off. Neither of them, I'm sure, remembered I had asked them about their values and their plan for retirement only a few months earlier during our initial meeting. Just as in that first conversation, they weren't sure where to begin.

Using the tools I outlined for you in our first retirement stepping-stone, I walked Joe and Susan through the process of identifying their values as individuals and as a married couple. A few things quickly became apparent:

Joe	Susan	Joe + Susan
Joe valued personal development. When he lived in Ohio year-round and had a full-time career, he felt like he was constantly working on improving himself. He was part of a cycling group, led a team at work, and regularly attended conferences to expand his knowledge about his industry.	Susan valued adventure and creativity. In her previous career, she had worked in a fast-paced office environment and enjoyed that things constantly shifted and changed. She loved traveling to new places frequently and learning new things.	Together, Joe and Susan valued community and their faith. Of course, they also valued time together and the connection with each other.

The Problem

Joe and Susan lived in a condo for half the year in an area of Arizona they loved. However, retirement had created several major problems for both of them individually and as a couple:

- Joe missed the personal development he had enjoyed back home. He hadn't found a way in Arizona to comfortably replace the leadership and growth he experienced at work. Additionally, without the consistency of cycling with his group, he had all but stopped exercising. He was spending most of his day in the condo watching TV or puttering around their new home fixing odds and ends.

- Susan had completely stopped incorporating any element of creativity into her life. She was no longer doing the kind of problem-solving she had done at work, and her pace of life had notably slowed down. Plus, since the move, she and Joe hadn't traveled or explored the area around their new home as they would have had they just been visiting.

- Joe and Susan didn't know anyone in their new neighborhood and weren't sure how to connect locally. They didn't enjoy the church near their condo and felt incredibly isolated.

The Solution

Joe and Susan didn't realize that though they were living their dream retirement, their new lifestyle actually conflicted with their values. By walking through this values exercise, they quickly realized that simply being retired and living in Arizona wasn't a sustainable or fulfilling lifestyle.

Together, we brainstormed a solution that would help solve their unhappiness. We began by looking at their condo. It had checked all of the boxes but wasn't helping them access the community or get involved in a local church in a way they would like.

Although they had bought it recently, they ended up selling their condo and purchasing a small home in a nearby retirement community. The new community still had a neighborhood HOA that took care of their property year-round, but they were now able to attend community events and establish relationships with other retirees who shared their same love of community and connection. The new retirement community was closer to a church they enjoyed, and they started attending it regularly.

We were able to adjust their financial plan to incorporate the sale of their condo and the purchase of this new property. Although the new home was slightly more expensive, the amenities it offered meant that Joe and Susan were less likely to spend money on entertainment and events outside of their community. This trade-off aligned with their values and therefore wasn't a problem.

Joe was able to find a local cycling group within the

retirement community, and he also connected with a men's small-group Bible study at their new church—successfully fulfilling his need for personal development and growth.

Susan loved that their new community offered courses (fitness, art, and so on) and was closer to the small downtown center of their new town. She was able to exercise her creativity and seek out new adventures by exploring their more accessible area.

Arizona ended up being the ideal solution for Joe and Susan. However, if they had continued to stay in their condo, they likely would never have found a financially sustainable and fulfilling life there. This is why it's so important to focus on aligning your ideal retirement lifestyle with your values. When your decisions are rooted in what's most important to you, you're more likely to feel fulfilled and live each retirement day with a sense of contentment.

How You Can Align Your Goals and Values

To turn Stumbling Block #3 into Stepping-Stone #3, take your list of values and the ideas you have for your ideal retirement, and see if they match up.

For example, if you value adventure and are planning to prioritize travel in retirement, make sure you focus on that in your budget because travel will make you feel fulfilled.

However, if you value community and family, but your

big goal for retirement is to travel the country for most of the year in a new RV, you probably won't be as content. In this scenario, you'd be largely separated from family and friends. If you do love to travel, you'll need to find a way to do it that aligns with your values. For example, perhaps you could coordinate a low-cost family reunion in a new fun (close-to-home) location each year.

By thinking ahead, you're setting yourself up for greater emotional and financial success in retirement.

What to Do If You're Burned Out

Experiencing burnout? You're not alone. You might be struggling with the idea of aligning a retirement lifestyle with your values because, right now, all you can think about is *not* going to work each day. In these situations, it's best to take what is called a "halftime." We've talked about halftime, as explained in Bob Buford's book, in a previous chapter, but it's worth reiterating the idea here.

Buford recommends that, although this new chapter of your life can be an exciting catalyst for change and living a life of significance, it's still important to build in a breather. When you first retire, take some time for yourself. Plan a year (or more, if needed) to simply be retired. Book a vacation. Spend time with your kids and grandkids. But have a plan for what comes *after* this halftime break. This, I believe, is where my mom went wrong in her planning.

She was ready to be retired but hadn't thought about what life would look like when she was rested, recharged, and ready to reengage. Mom had always been a doer, and she likely needed to get back to *something* sooner than she had anticipated.

Many retirees think they may spend 5–10 years living a leisurely life when they first retire. However, that isn't always true. Mom enjoyed her new lifestyle only for a few weeks, or a few months at most, before exhibiting signs of depression.

Remember, taking a break can be part of your plan. Just remember that when you're ready to move on and reengage, you need to have the next steps in place to help you continue living a purposeful life.

Chapter 8

BUILDING COMMUNITY

Stumbling Block #4: Loss of Community

As you enter retirement, you may find that your community slowly slips away. After all, whether you realize it or not, many of your connections likely come from your workplace or career. Whether you spend time with coworkers outside of work or not, you're still spending 8–12 hours each day with them Monday through Friday.

That's 40–60 hours a week, or 24–36 percent of your time. Considering that you likely spend almost the same amount of time (or more) sleeping and eating, it's safe to say that the majority of your *waking* hours are spent with coworkers.

For some, this is a good thing. For example, I love my

job, and I love the team I work with! As an entrepreneur and a partner in my wealth-management firm, I've helped to build a business that I enjoy and that includes the people I spend a lot of my time with.

However, even in cases when you may not love your coworkers, you may be underestimating the large role they play in your life. My mom loved her team, and she loved the patients she worked with. Over time, though, some of her closest colleagues and work friends slowly started to leave. They retired, found other jobs, moved away—and she was quickly left with a career that she wasn't in love with anymore.

She didn't think that she would miss her team, especially because she was so excited to stop work and spend more time with my dad, the grandkids, and my sister. She was also ready to spend more time with various groups she belonged to at her church and with her friends outside of work. In other words, she had what she assumed was a strong community that she was ready to connect with more deeply.

Then retirement hit.

Even though the nonwork community she had cherished was still there, those people didn't have 8–12 hours a day to spend time with her. My dad was still working and hadn't made the jump to full-time retirement yet. My wife, Keri, and I were growing our young family; and Net and her husband, Mark, still had jobs and lives of their own. We were all looking forward to spending more time with Mom when she retired, but it wasn't enough to meet the 8–12 hours, five days a week, that she had been used to.

Her experience, unfortunately, isn't unique. You can have the strongest, most loving, supportive community in the entire world, and that doesn't necessarily mean those folks will be able to fill your calendar in the future.

Retirement Stepping-Stone #4: Building a Retirement Support System

For this reason, it's incredibly important that pre-retirees start to think about who they want to connect with, and how, before they completely give up work. Knowing in advance that you not only have a support system but also a group of people you can connect with in a meaningful way in your new lifestyle can have a colossal positive impact.

Building Your Community in Advance

"We cannot live only for ourselves. A thousand fibers connect us with our fellow men," said Herman Melville. Indeed, scientifically and spiritually, we are not made to be alone. There is a reason we were put on this earth together—it's to connect with one another and find growth and contentment in community, all while living out our purpose. For most of us, community isn't tough to come by when we're younger. We're born into a family and, like them or not, they're what we're stuck with for a while.

Then, of course, there's the opportunity to make friends or even just school-day acquaintances all the way through college. You might play sports, join a community organization or club, attend a faith-based organization, get your first job, or do any number of other things that grow your community further.

As a young adult, you may start your own family and begin to grow your career. It seems that every step you take surrounds you with an even bigger network of people to socialize with. Not everyone in your network is going to be an ideal fit for you, but that doesn't mean they don't serve a purpose: They are connected to you, just as you are to them.

Retirement throws a wrench in this organic community-building cycle. You go from finding natural ways to connect with others to being relatively isolated in short order. Worse yet, you're doing this during a relatively turbulent time of your life. Because you've always been surrounded by a natural network, it's uncomfortable to suddenly be ripped from it—and to be expected to build your own.

Luckily, there are several steps you can take to maintain connection postretirement. Let's talk about which members in your community may be valuable during this new chapter.

A Social Group

A social group isn't a single individual you can add to your community roster, but it's still useful to think about before you actually retire. Finding a social group that's dedicated to a hobby you love or a cause you're passionate about can help you to transition relatively easily to your new normal. A social group can serve as a kind of replacement for the everyday work community that you're leaving. For example, if you leave your full-time job but immediately join a book club that meets weekly or a volunteer group that coordinates your local farmers market throughout the week, you'll be able to replace some of the time you spent with your colleagues with a new, organic segment of your ever-growing community.

My advice is not to wait until retirement to find a few group options that may work for you. Do research ahead of time, and maybe even test out certain groups on the weekends while you're still employed. Get to know volunteers or members of different local groups or organizations, and determine what's going to be the best fit for you.

A Mentor

It's wise to look back through your network to find a mentor—someone you like and respect who has already made the transition to retirement. This person can help guide you through your own journey and offer insights as you run into emotional roadblocks. This person can be an older friend or sibling or even a coworker who retired before you.

In fact, the more connections you can make with retirees *before* you retire, the better. Although you may find that staying consistently connected to your still-employed friends is easy after retirement, this is not always the case. They are, after all, at a different stage of life than you are. Friendships have their seasons, and you may struggle to keep in close contact with former coworkers if they don't have your schedule or just aren't as available to connect as you are.

This won't be the case with friends or family who have already retired. By connecting with these people in advance, you're building a segment of your community that is having similar experiences to you and will have a similar schedule. You'll be able to grab coffee during the workweek to catch up or spend time together whenever is convenient for you. I've often seen social groups who are all currently retired truly thrive because they're all able to dedicate so much time and energy to themselves and one another. Relationships grow well in that type of environment!

Family

You may think that adding "family" to your list of community members is redundant. *Aren't they already part of your community?* Yes and no.

Your close family will always be there for you, but it's worth reengaging with them before retiring. Even if you feel genuinely ready to retire and aren't worried about depression or the retirement blues in the slightest, it's still wise to reach out preemptively. This is partly because you may struggle with an identity shift that changes the way you wish to connect to your family. It's also because family members may not recognize your changed needs during this transition because, for them, life hasn't changed.

For example, when Mom retired, she was excited to spend more time with her grandkids and Dad. As my own family grew, I was excited to see her in her role as grandma. I pictured her coming over to see our kids, spending time with me, Keri, and Net, and taking long-weekend vacations with Dad. For the most part, she felt the same. Everyone in our family, Mom included, felt that life would just continue to be business as usual— even though now we know it wasn't.

However, if she had reached out directly before retiring and asked those who were closest to her for extra support, we may have been aware of the seriousness of her issues a bit sooner. If we had been alerted to the fact that she may have needed extra support, her transition to retirement could have been much smoother.

I'm not saying that reaching out to your family before retirement will counteract possible depression or make everything right. I'm also not saying that you *have to* rely on your family as you go through a transitional season.

Still, even if reconnecting with your family simply makes your community a little bit stronger and more supportive during this time, isn't that worth it?

I find these conversations are especially important to have with your adult kids or siblings as you enter retirement—especially if they're still working. Taking note of the fact that your life is changing, even when theirs is not, can help to wake them up to the very real possibility that you may need them and their love a little more than usual.

Friends

Whether you have friends through work or through other parts of your life, now is the time to reconnect with them. Strengthening your relationship with friends you're currently close to—or those you have fallen out of touch with—only increases the total number of people who are available to connect with you and fosters a sense of community. A few ideas for connecting before retirement might be:

- Asking an old work colleague out for coffee

- Reaching out to a friend you haven't spoken with in a while to see how he or she is doing

- Connecting more frequently with members of a social group you're part of

- Scheduling a couples' dinner for you, your spouse, and friends

- Inviting a group of people over for a potluck-style dinner party at your house

You don't have to connect with people just to alert them to the fact that you're retiring and want to build your community. That might feel awkward or even presumptuous. Instead, think outside of the box to build social engagements into your schedule in a creative way. These moments will be the launchpad for your ongoing relationships in the future.

A Counselor

If you've never worked with a certified counselor or therapist, locating one now may seem intimidating. However, this is absolutely the time to find a professional you trust. Taking care of your mental health during this transition is of the utmost importance, and checking in with someone who is trained to do just that is wise. You don't have to be depressed to seek therapy.

You don't need to be suffering from anxiety or experiencing marital struggles. Just as you would go to a doctor for a checkup or a physical exam, you can absolutely connect with a therapist or counselor just to take a look "under the hood" and make sure you're healthy.

You can find a therapist or counselor in several different ways:

1. **Ask your loved ones.** Seriously—you'll be surprised to find out exactly who goes to therapy and loves their therapist if you just ask. This is far more common than you may think. It's important to talk to others about working with a therapist; caring for one's mental health needs should be considered a normal part of life.

2. **Find an online directory.** Sites like *Psychology Today* can help you find local counselors or therapists in your area.

3. **Ask your doctor.** Your primary-care physician will likely have several recommendations for you; just ask.

4. **Think about your purpose.** If you find a therapist online and you aren't sure the person is a great fit, reach out and be clear about your purpose. Explain the life transition you're about to go through, and ask if identity shifts or transitions are something they help clients with or if they do not—and this is key—*if they have any referrals*. Most therapists do not take on clients who fall outside of their zone of expertise. If they can't help you, they likely know someone else who can.

A Pastor or Faith-Based Community

If you are a person of faith, or once were, but haven't been to your place of worship for a while, reaching out to a pastor or your faith community leader can help during this time of your life. I know that my mom found a lot of solace talking with her pastor during retirement, and I truly believe that he helped her navigate through some difficult emotions.

Reaching out to your pastor or religious leader/mentor can help you ground yourself in something you genuinely value. This player on your retirement-community roster can be invaluable and shouldn't be overlooked.

Bonus: Ask Your Community Questions

Take the time to ask the members of your growing community meaningful questions. These will help you shape your social engagements during retirement and set clear expectations moving forward.

Questions for Friends

- Would you be interested in starting a group to do [insert hobby or passion project here]?

- What's your availability to spend time together?

- Would you want to attend [insert event—faith community, concert, book reading, movie] with me?

Questions for Family

For children:

- How involved would you like me to be in your/ your kids' lives now that I'm retired?

- Do you have any expectations of me now that I'm retired? (You don't want to find out after you've retired that your kids expected you to babysit every weekend—especially if that wasn't in your plans!)

For spouse or partner:

- How do you envision us spending our retirement?

- Do you want to spend the majority of our time together, or would you like to be involved in social groups or communities on your own?

- Do we plan to retire together?

Remember, when it comes to family, don't count on underlying assumptions. Starting these conversations is 95 percent of the battle, but having them before your retirement can help to head off any unpleasant mismatched expectations.

Questions for a Pastor or Counselor/Therapist

- I'm having some fears about [insert retirement fear]; can we talk?

- How can I ground myself during a season that feels uncertain?

Your community is your number-one asset in retirement, and building it up before retirement can help you make the transition significantly easier.

Connected Connie

When Connie retired, she knew she'd miss her job and work environment. She had worked as an accountant at a small, local firm for 30 years. She had enjoyed her time there as a senior accountant and spent most of her working days training new hires and meeting with top-level clients. Her favorite part of her job was the people she worked with. Connie loved everyone on her team and felt that many of her clients were close friends.

Before retiring, Connie set out to cement some of these connections outside of the office so that she wouldn't have to disconnect from the people she cared about. She reached out to a few key clients who had been with the firm for years and knew of her upcoming retirement, and scheduled lunch dates to chat and catch up. She also made a point of hosting a few small dinner gatherings at her home with the coworkers who she had grown closest to. It felt good to be connected with these wonderful people at the office and even better knowing that she would be able to remain friends with them after retiring.

Connie took it a step further and looked closely at her nonwork community. She knew that, realistically, her coworkers and clients couldn't spend Tuesday afternoons with her sipping coffee at a local bookshop or catching an afternoon matinee. She'd need a circle of friends and loved ones whose schedules matched her own.

With this in mind, Connie moved through her community list and jotted down the people who she knew she wanted to foster a closer relationship with now that her time wasn't dedicated to work. Her social group and friends consisted of her old coworkers, clients, and several friends from the book club she'd been helping to run for the past few years.

She reached out to her older sister who had retired three years earlier as a mentor figure, asking questions about making the retirement transition and what she might expect. Connie had always been close with her family, but she took time before retiring to sit down with her son and daughter-in-law over lunch. She knew she wanted to be more involved in her grandchildren's lives but certainly didn't want to overstep. She was relieved to hear that her kids welcomed her interest in being more present, and they all planned to get together more consistently for family outings on weekends.

Finally, Connie knew that it was critical for her to get both her mental and spiritual health in order before making the transition to retirement. Any life change is generally challenging to get used to, and even though she was excited about what was ahead of her, she was also nervous about taking the leap. Connie connected with a counselor who had helped her navigate her divorce in the past and reached out to a friend who was part of a local church's women's group. She knew that having this extra level of support would be invaluable during this time.

As you can see in this example, building a strong community heading into retirement doesn't have to be overly time-consuming or challenging. You don't have to go out of your way to make new connections or try and build new hobbies or relationships. Taking a few different lunches or afternoons to connect often with people you already know and love is enough to solidify your retirement community.

Chapter 9

TAKING ACTIONABLE STEPS BEFORE RETIREMENT

Stumbling Block #5: You're Unhappy with Your Retirement Lifestyle

How many times have you planned for an ideal vacation for weeks or months—only to feel a little bit underwhelmed when you actually arrived at your destination?

Too often, we spend a lot of time and energy planning for things we want. Take the vacation example. We may pass the hours dreaming of:

- The perfect location

- An ideal itinerary

- The cool family memories we'll make

- The social-media-worthy pictures we might take with our loved ones

- Places to go and sights to see

- Foods we want to eat

- How we'll describe the trip to our friends

- How we'll feel after we get home—rested and relaxed

- Staying within our budget

Unfortunately, life rarely goes exactly as planned. The restaurant you researched and made reservations at may have changed its menu. The social-media pictures you imagined may not pan out if the weather is grayer than you had anticipated. Maybe you had your heart set on visiting a particular pristine beach, only to realize that it's packed with tourists!

In short, sometimes, when we spend so much time imagining what our vacation *might be like*, we're disappointed with reality. We've wasted so much energy idealizing an experience that we don't have the capacity or mind-set to enjoy what's going on in the moment.

Planning your retirement is often like planning a really fun vacation. Many people I speak with in my role as a financial advisor are incredibly excited about retirement.

They've planned it down to every detail. They imagine themselves buying a boat, golfing, refinishing their home, traveling, enjoying time with family—living their ideal lifestyle every single day of retirement. The truth is that this rarely happens for a variety of reasons. Just as an "ideal vacation" can turn out not quite as planned, your "ideal retirement" may not be everything you've dreamed of.

Retirement Stepping-Stone #5: Build a Retirement Lifestyle You Love before You Retire

Let's talk about some of the reasons why the retirement you're imagining might not go according to plan and what you can do about it.

Problem: Your Dream Retirement Is Too Expensive

Sometimes the retirement you imagine isn't the retirement you can actually afford. While you might be picturing yourself relaxing on a beach while you are a snowbird for half of the year in Florida, you may lack the funds to make that dream a reality. Sometimes, when presented with the truth of retirement and the need to continue to live within their means, retirees can start to feel deflated and depressed.

Actionable Step: Think ahead to build a retirement plan and dream within your financial limits. The more realistic you are with yourself about your budget and how that translates to your retirement lifestyle, the more content you will be.

If it looks like you may not be able to financially sustain your lifestyle in retirement, take steps ahead of time to reduce your expenses. For example, many people choose to downsize in retirement to pay off their mortgage and cut part of their budget. Making this move before you retire can mean more time to:

- Get used to the new size of your home with your spouse or partner.

- Make your new space feel like *you*. If you downsize before you retire, you can decorate the new place, identify home improvement projects you want to tackle postretirement, and get used to the change.

- Save more money prior to retirement. Without a mortgage payment, you can funnel more money into your retirement savings, making it possible to live the lifestyle you want when it actually comes time to retire.

Frugal Fran

Like many people, Fran had spent the majority of her life imagining what retirement would be like. In her mind's eye, she pictured spending summers in Greece or Italy, coming home to her cozy cabin in the Tennessee mountains, and still finding time and resources to travel for extended periods of time to visit her daughter and son-in-law in Ohio. When it came time to crunch the numbers, however, she realized there was no feasible way to accomplish the lavish lifestyle she had imagined in retirement.

Fran, never one to be deterred, set to work figuring out the best way to align her limited resources in retirement with the dreams she had previously held. After doing some soul searching, she determined that she had three primary desires for her retirement lifestyle:

1. **To spend time with family.** Spending time with her daughter and son-in-law during her retirement was Fran's number-one priority. She decided that, even though she'd always imagined retiring to a cozy little cabin in the mountains of Tennessee, she'd be just as happy staying put in Ohio to be closer to them.

2. **To travel.** Even though it was certainly one of the more expensive goals she had set for retirement, Fran knew she couldn't give up her dream of traveling the world. This meant she'd have to trim

expenses elsewhere. She'd already decided that buying property and a cabin in Tennessee wasn't in her plans, but the numbers still didn't add up.

3. **To enjoy the limited time spent at home in a space where she felt comfortable.** Fran realized that if she wanted to spend time abroad and visiting her family, she didn't need the 2,000-square-foot house she had been living in since her daughter was a child. She was still paying down her mortgage and decided to reach out to a realtor to see how much she could feasibly list her home for. Once she determined that she'd make a tidy profit on the sale of her home, she put it on the market and started looking for a smaller, more manageable, one-bedroom condo to buy outright. Without a mortgage payment, she'd be able to put more money aside for travel before retiring, and she wouldn't have to worry about the upkeep of a large home when she was abroad.

Problem: You've Only Imagined the Highlight Reel

This is all too common for pre-retirees. If you're about to retire and you only imagine the stellar moments, you might not be excited to realize that every day won't live up to your bucket-list moments. Think about your life before retirement. Every day isn't a vacation or a magical weekend at a big family reunion making lasting memories. Those moments, in reality, are few and far between.

Actionable Step: Test out what average retirement might look like for you, and plan ahead for how you'll spend your time. For example, you might take a week off and simply live your life. Try out a staycation to see if you enjoy your current home and whether you can find enough activities to keep you occupied and content.

If you find yourself bored or a little purposeless, think through what you might enjoy spending your time doing when you retire. Do you want to pick up a new hobby? Are you interested in volunteer work, or do you want to dedicate your next few years to a passion project in your community? Take actionable steps to make these lifestyle changes before you actually retire so that you have something to retire *to*—not just a career to retire *from*.

Staycation Steve

Steve had his retirement bucket list planned out years before he was even close to leaving his career as a bank branch manager. He was going to:

- Take time to golf the top 10 courses in the country.

- Spend at least one week a year vacationing somewhere tropical with his wife, Jan.

- Redo his backyard to include a pool for his grandkids.

These plans were exciting, but they didn't take into account the fact that he wouldn't be golfing every day for the next 10–40 years! Steve hadn't truly considered this, but before retiring, Steve decided to take a staycation to "test-drive" what his daily life would look like. The very first day, Steve panicked. He had no idea how he wanted to spend his morning, let alone the next five days of vacation. Steve immediately knew there was a gap in his planning: He wasn't sure how he wanted to spend his daily life.

Steve sat down with Jan that evening. He expressed his concerns, and she grabbed a pen and a notebook. Together, they talked through what was most important to them and how they wanted to spend their time. They took note of what they enjoyed (and what they didn't enjoy) about their current lifestyle. What quickly became apparent was that their favorite activity to do together was to work on home-improvement projects, including spending time in their expansive garden and greenhouse.

Although Steve had originally planned to retire a year ahead of Jan, they ultimately decided it would be wise to hold off for another year. Steve couldn't imagine waiting around the house all day while Jan went to work as an elementary school teacher, and they knew that if they retired together, they'd both be happier and less lonely. They made plans to continue expanding their knowledge of gardening by taking a course or two online prior to retirement, and Jan suggested that Steve start to research what it might look like to have a booth at the local farmers market in the summers. With this new plan, Steve felt confident that he'd not only be able to accomplish the exciting travel and home renovations he'd planned for but also enjoy his daily life.

Problem: You Were Desperate to Get Out of Your Career

I truly believe that had my mom not felt so burned out at her job in hospice care, she could have eased into retirement more prepared for the big lifestyle changes she was about to face. However, because she was exhausted, she dove into retirement headfirst without thinking through whether she was emotionally ready to make the transition.

Although my parents were financially stable, my mom was always worried that they wouldn't have enough money after she retired. Beyond that, she felt like her career had given her purpose. Without financial stability or career-driven personal fulfillment, she was lost and fell into depression.

Actionable Step: Had my mom chosen to test-drive retirement before plunging in, she might have been more content and better prepared for any emotional stressors she was bound to face. One thing that may help pre-retirees who are burned out make this retirement transition smoother is to consider working part time before stopping completely.

When you're burned out, there are usually several reasons for it:

- You're working long hours.

- You're uncomfortable with changes in your work environment.

- Your colleagues are leaving or changing.

- You don't feel your skill set is keeping pace with changing demands.

- You're overworked or are expected to take on too many responsibilities in your role.

Although change can be challenging for pre-retirees who have built careers they're proud of, going part time at work before fully retiring can offer several benefits. First and foremost, reducing the amount that you're working can help you to recover from burnout and exhaustion. Working part time may mean a reduction in your responsibilities, but you won't be fully sacrificing work that you found fulfilling at some point in your career.

Once you're reenergized by part-time work, you may find that you are, in fact, ready to retire. However, if you find that you are happy with your current amount of work and with the type of work you're doing, you may have the clarity of mind to stay on for a while longer. This can lead to a number of personally fulfilling benefits.

Part-Time Peg

Peg was exhausted at her job. She had been the CFO at a small marketing firm for the past 10 years and was burned out. It wasn't that she didn't love her coworkers or the work she was doing; she just felt incredibly stuck. The passion she had once felt for ensuring that the business ran a tight financial ship was dwindling quickly. Many days, all she could think about was waking up the morning after her retirement party. She'd sleep in, never change out of her pajamas, and spend a lazy afternoon reading books on her screened porch with her cat, Max.

Gearing up for retirement consumed most of Peg's time, and she started to get tunnel vision. She saved aggressively, spoke to the C-Suite at her office about her imminent retirement to ensure everyone was aware of and prepared for her departure, and even started spending her weekends researching local retirement social groups that she could join. As part of her focused planning, Peg decided to grab lunch with a friend who had retired a year earlier; Joe had been one of the co-owners of a local graphic design firm who had put together her company's website.

Peg was excited to hear about what Joe was up to and wanted to hear firsthand whether retirement was as amazing as she had always imagined it to be. At their lunch, Peg was surprised to find Joe more than a little frazzled. He admitted that, while he enjoyed spending time at home with his wife and loved getting to see his grandkids more often, he missed the office. Peg was shocked. How could he miss the hustle and bustle of the workplace? Small businesses can be fraught with ups and downs, and the pressure to always perform and keep the business growing can be overwhelming.

Joe agreed, but he explained that he missed the interactions he had at work. He loved the work he had been doing and felt lost without the purpose that comes with being part of a small team. On her drive home, Peg thought about what Joe had said. The next day, she went into work and spoke with her colleagues about possibly working part time for a few years to train her assistant, Sarah, to take over as CFO. The entire team was relieved. Peg's expertise was invaluable, and the CEO even said he'd be interested in having her stay on in a consulting capacity after Sarah was fully trained. This new vision of retirement allowed Peg the flexibility to set her own schedule and step out of the day-to-day business but still continue to do the work she loved with people she enjoyed.

Problem: You Didn't Test the Lifestyle Adjustments

Many retirees plan to move to a new neighborhood, spend winters in a sunnier location, or make other dramatic lifestyle changes once they enter retirement. However, doing this can often mean that you're tackling two major changes at once:

1. Your retirement

2. Your new lifestyle shift

Actionable Step: Consider testing out any potential change you are considering for your retirement before you actually take the leap. For example, if you're thinking about relocating, you may be able to rent a place on a site like Airbnb or VRBO and stay there in the long term while working remotely. Spend several weeks (or months) in your new location. Get used to the grocery store, test out local restaurants or gyms, and get a general idea of what life would be like if you lived there.

Taking this step prior to retirement can help you understand the reality of the decision you plan to make and let you decide whether it's a good fit for you.

Careful Carl

Carl knew that when retirement came, he'd be ready for a change. His wife had passed away a few years earlier, and he didn't enjoy the idea of spending time alone in their home. He had several friends who had retired recently and moved to the greater Phoenix area. He lived in the Midwest, and the idea of a mild winter and year-round sunshine were incredibly appealing. Carl had been to visit his retired friends several times over the past few years and had all but chosen his ideal neighborhood and packed his bags.

Then Carl decided to take a step back and test-drive the Phoenix lifestyle. His friends enjoyed it, and he loved spending time there when traveling. But would he miss the midwestern fall and winter days? What would it look like to live in an entirely different state?

Carl decided to rent a condo for a few weeks and work remotely near the retirement community where many of his friends lived and where he planned to buy. After only a few days, Carl realized that, while he loved Phoenix, the original neighborhoods he had in mind didn't have any of the amenities he would look for in daily life. The retirement communities his friends lived in were lovely and well-kept but lacked easy access to the great outdoors, and he didn't like many of the local grocery stores and restaurants. Carl realized that vacationing in Arizona to escape the midwestern winter was dramatically different than having to live there year-round. About a week into his stay, Carl drove to a friend's house in Flagstaff a few hours away. He hadn't visited in the past because all his other Arizona-based friends had been in Phoenix. He'd had limited time to truly explore the state of Arizona.

As he got closer to Flagstaff, however, Carl felt the knot in his stomach loosen. The mountains in the area were beautiful. After he arrived at his friend's, Carl was amazed to hear about everything the area had to offer. The Grand Canyon was within driving distance, and other activities including outdoor hiking were readily available. Although Flagstaff had different weather than Phoenix, it was still better than the icy Midwest. Carl decided Flagstaff was his ideal retirement location.

Had he not taken the extended trip and spent time exploring different areas of his dream location, Carl might have retired to Phoenix only to realize he hated the area when it was too late to do anything about it. By being careful and planning, Carl was able to reimagine a retirement he would truly love.

Taking Actionable Steps

If you commit to building the retirement lifestyle you love before retirement actually starts, you're also committing to making the transition much smoother for you and your family. Regardless of what you have planned for retirement, these actions can help you construct a lifestyle you're looking forward to and sidestep any unpleasant surprises.

Chapter 10

FINANCIAL PLANNING AND RETIREMENT SAVINGS

Stumbling Block #6: You're Not Sure If You're Financially Ready for Retirement

Are you ready to retire? We've spent a lot of time in this book talking about whether or not you're *emotionally* ready for retirement and prepared to navigate the lifestyle change once you take the leap. I truly believe that not gearing up emotionally for the retirement transition is one of the number-one stumbling blocks that people encounter. However, I'd be remiss if we didn't spend time discussing another way you need to prepare for this next chapter in your life: You have to have a financial plan.

The Psychology of Finances in Retirement

The truth is that retirement is difficult in more ways than one. For a variety of reasons, many people struggle with some sort of depression when going through this lifestyle change. For example, my mom found that going from working and finding fulfillment in her career to staying at home in retirement was incredibly difficult. I also know how concerned she was about her finances.

When my parents were ready to retire, they had their primary financial planner and me give them the green light. If they continued to live frugally, we both advised them, they would be able to live comfortably for the rest of their lives as retirees.

Even so, the first week Mom retired, she started to panic. I remember her pacing the floor, talking to various family members about how she and my dad were going to run out of money. Given my business experience, I was able to reassure her countless times that this wasn't the case. However, the truth is that many retirees face a similar, unfounded anxiety about their finances when they leave their careers behind.

The difference is due to the huge mental shift required to go from accumulation to dispersal. In other words, seeing your account balances go down instead of up is scary.

You've spent your entire life and career saving; you've saved for retirement, a down payment for a house, vacations, an emergency fund, a new car, college tuition for kids (and maybe grandkids). Making the switch to spending down the large amount of money you've saved often goes against your better judgment. This is why it's especially important to have an airtight financial plan that prioritizes your ideal lifestyle, your values, and something for a legacy. Let's talk about how to put a retirement plan together.

Retirement Stepping-Stone #6: Build an Airtight Retirement Budget

Know Your Number

The first step in successful retirement planning is to know your number. In other words, how much money do you need to have saved in order to comfortably retire? There are several equations that can help you estimate what this number might be. These rules of thumb are:

- 80–90 percent of your pre-retirement income

- $1 million

- 12 times your pre-retirement income

- 25 times your desired living expenses

While all of these ballpark figures are useful to help you get started and to have something to aim for, they are rarely accurate. The truth is that you need to reverse-engineer your retirement number to make sure there will be enough for you.

Start with Spending

How much do you plan on spending in retirement? Start by looking at your current expenses. Be honest with yourself when doing this. Estimating how much you spend is a great starting point, but going back to examine your actual spending habits is critical. You can do this by checking your bank or credit card statements.

You can also choose to use an app like *You Need a Budget* or *Mint* to track your spending for several months. How much are your total average monthly expenses? Once you have this number, write it down.

Example: Monthly expenses are $5,000.

Some of your expenses will change in retirement. For example, you may spend a significant amount of money commuting or paying for parking at your current job. In retirement, these expenses will likely go away. You may also know that some big expenses, like your mortgage, will be paid off once you retire.

However, you may also encounter new lifestyle expenses. For example, you may decide to join a country club so you can golf more often and enjoy a sense of community. Do your best to estimate what monthly expenses will go away and what recurring expenses may be added to your budget after you retire. Write this new number down.

Example: New monthly expense estimate (after removing work-related costs and adding daily retirement lifestyle expenses) is $4,500.

Multiply your average monthly expenses by 12.

$4,500 x 12 = $54,000

Now consider your current life expectancy. I always tell people it's wise to plan for a longer life than you may think is possible. The last thing you want is to live well past 90 and to have only planned a savings that supports you through age 80.

If you retire at 67 and estimate that you'll live to 100, that's a good start. Now, the financial advisor in me wants to do a fancy present-value calculation and factor in inflation, but for purposes of this example, we'll stick with simple math. So multiply your annual baseline expenses by your total years in retirement.

$54,000 x 33 = $1,782,000

Now that you have your average expenses mapped out, you can start thinking outside the box. Retirees have two major expenses that they often forget to build into their budget:

- Health expenses
- Bucket-list expenses

Start with your estimated health expenses. The average retired couple needs to have $295,000 saved for health or medical expenses in retirement (according to the Fidelity Retiree Health Care Cost Estimate[7]). If you have preexisting conditions or a family history of medical problems that require long-term care, you may end up spending more. Speak with your physician about the best way to prepare for potential medical problems in retirement, and use the baseline figure of $295,000 to help estimate what you'll need to set aside to pay for your medical expenses.

Next, move to your bucket-list expenses. What big, exciting plans do you have to spend money on during retirement? For example, let's say you are planning to buy a boat and take one extended vacation with your spouse each year. The up-front cost of your boat is $40,000. Ongoing upkeep and storage for your boat is approximately $5,000 per year. Your annual vacations average $6,000 per trip.

7   "Planning for Health Care Costs in Retirement," Fidelity, accessed February 6, 2021, https://institutional.fidelity.com/app/item/ RD_13569_42402/retirement-planning-health-care-costs.html.

Add both your medical expense estimate and your bucket-list expenses to your total retirement-savings estimate.

$1,782,000 + Medical ($295,000) + Boat ($205,000) + Travel ($198,000) = $2,480,000

You can see here that by reverse-engineering your retirement-savings goal, you're able to get a much more accurate estimate of what you should expect to spend over the course of your retirement. This can help set you up for success when trying to save.

Chapter 11

UNDERSTAND YOUR RETIREMENT INCOME

Stumbling Block #7: You Don't Know How to Use Your Savings to Fund Your Retirement Lifestyle

Let's say you have your total expense estimate and are using it as a ballpark savings goal. That's great! Now, you need to take a deeper dive into how you will recreate a paycheck in retirement to pay for your expenses. Most people's retirement income comes from a combination of places:

- Qualified retirement accounts (your 401k, for example)

- Nonqualified retirement accounts (like your Roth IRA)

- Pension

- Social Security

- HSA

Let's explore how you can create income from each of these sources during retirement.

Retirement Stepping-Stone #7: Understand Your Retirement Income

Qualified Retirement Accounts

A qualified retirement account is a retirement-savings account that was funded with pretax dollars during your career. This might be a 401k, 403b, traditional IRA, or a 457 plan, depending on your employer and industry. Because these accounts are funded with pretax dollars, they are taxable in retirement. Distributions from these accounts are taxed at normal income tax rates.

The nice thing about qualified savings accounts is that they're incredibly prevalent in the American workforce. Most companies will offer some kind of tax-deferred retirement account that you can fund directly from your paycheck. This allows you to both save for your future retirement and, because these accounts are funded with pretax dollars, to reduce your current taxable income.

Additionally, many employers offer a matching program up to a certain percentage of your income. For example, your employer may match 100 percent of your contributions up to 6 percent of your total income. By contributing up to your employer match, you're guaranteeing yourself "free money" from your employer toward your retirement savings.

When you retire and reach age 59½, you are allowed access to your qualified retirement accounts. In fact, you *have* to take a certain amount of money out of these accounts each year after age 72. This is called your Required Minimum Distribution (RMD). In other words, the government requires that you take an RMD each year from your account to force you to pay the tax. This RMD is calculated by taking your total account balance on December 31 of the previous year multiplied by a life expectancy factor determined by the IRS. It should be noted that in 2020, due to the coronavirus pandemic, RMDs were suspended. This is a rare occurrence (the last time RMDs were suspended was during the Global Financial Crisis for the year 2009) and shows that future RMDs may also be suspended depending on the global climate.

Nonqualified Retirement Accounts

Nonqualified retirement accounts are funded with money that has already been taxed. This could be a Roth IRA, Roth 401k, or another type of investment account funded outside of your employer. Because these accounts are funded with money that's already been taxed, you won't owe taxes on distributions from the accounts during retirement.

For many people, funding nonqualified accounts makes sense because their income-tax bracket now is much lower than what it would be when they finally retire. Assuming you will continue to receive pay increases over the course of your career, this may be true for you as well. The most popular nonqualified account you can set up is a Roth IRA.

However, there are some limitations regarding who can contribute to a Roth IRA. As a result, many people think that contributing to a Roth IRA isn't appropriate for them and that they can't take advantage of the tax benefits. Be sure to check with your financial advisor before making a contribution.

This is where a backdoor Roth IRA may come into play.

Some individuals choose to convert a portion of their 401k, or other qualified retirement savings account, to their Roth IRA each year. Performing a conversion isn't restricted by your annual income. This means you could potentially fund a nonqualified retirement savings account by converting funds from your qualified accounts annually.

Of course, when you perform this action, you must pay taxes on the funds you convert based on your current income tax bracket. Keep in mind that these funds can now be counted as taxable income and may impact which tax bracket you fall into.

Pension

Although pensions aren't as popular as they once were, many companies still offer an employee pension to all employees who have worked with them for a set number of years. Typically, your pension will vest (or become available to you) in small increments over several years in the beginning of your career. For example, you may be 50 percent vested after three years of service, 75 percent vested after five, and 100 percent vested by year seven.

If you're planning your retirement, you have several options for taking your pension. Determining which option is best for you depends on several factors:

- Whether you plan to invest the funds from your pension after retirement

- Whether you immediately need the funds from your pension after retirement

- Whether you have a spouse who may outlive you and will need financial assistance after you pass away

- How long you will live. I know—none of us have the answer to this, but you can make an educated guess based on family history, your own health, and your expected future lifestyle.

Here are the various pension options you may encounter at retirement:

Lump Sum

This option is exactly what it sounds like. You can request a lump sum of your pension at the onset of your retirement. This can be useful for retirees who need a cash injection to live comfortably in the early years of retirement or to pay off debt or for those who plan to invest the lump sum to continue accruing interest in the coming years.

Single-Life Annuity

This option will provide the largest monthly payments to the retiree. The payments will last as long as the retired employee lives. However, once the employee passes away, payments stop—even if the full pension hasn't been paid out.

Joint-and-Survivor Annuity

Usually joint-and-survivor options come with varying percentages available. This pension option gives you a reduced monthly payment while the retired employee is living, and that same reduced payment will continually be made to a surviving spouse after the retired employee passes away.

Period Certain

This pension option guarantees payments to be made to either the retired employee or a surviving spouse for a certain number of years, regardless of whether or not the retired employee passes away. For example, a period-certain option may guarantee payments for 20 years. Even if the retired employee lives beyond the first 20 years of retirement, the payments would not continue for the remainder of their lives. However, if the retired employee passes away 15 years into their retirement, the remaining five years of payments could go to a spouse or beneficiary.

Selecting a Pension Option

There is no right pension option. At the end of the day, each retiree needs to select a plan that will best suit his or her needs. For example, a widow who is entering retirement may be perfectly comfortable with a single-life-annuity option.

However, a retiree who has a spouse and adult children who could benefit from their pension payments may look to select a period-certain or joint-and-survivor option. If you have a pension, you need to determine how you will use the payments from your pension, and whether you and your family have enough savings outside of your pension to continue living comfortably if pension payments were to go away.

The most common pension selection is far and away a lump sum. This is because, often, retirees are interested in reinvesting their lump-sum payment. Lump-sum payments give the recipient the most control over their money. Even if the lump sum is slightly less than the total amount of annuity payments, you may be able to invest the funds in a way that's better for you and your unique lifestyle situation.

Social Security

Many retirees count on Social Security to be part of their retirement income. After all, you've paid into the program for the entirety of your career! While many retirees understand that they'll be receiving a Social Security benefit, there's often confusion about how much they'll receive and when.

In order to receive your Social Security benefits, you must enroll in Social Security once you hit a certain age. You are technically permitted to enroll after age 62. However, this is earlier than your full retirement age, so benefits will be reduced if you choose to enroll and receive a benefit early.

Your full retirement age is dependent on your birth year and could be anywhere from age 66 to age 67. For example, if you were born in 1956, your full retirement age is 66 and 4 months. You can find your full retirement age by visiting the Social Security Administration's website.

You also have the option to delay your Social Security benefit up to age 70. If you choose to delay your benefit, you will increase the total monthly payments you receive when you do finally enroll.

Health Savings Accounts (HSA)

Remember that we talked about how most couples over age 65 spend close to $300,000 on medical expenses in retirement? It's critical that you plan for how you want to cover those expenses. One option is a health savings account (HSA). If you have a high-deductible health plan (an insurance option) through your employer, you have access to your very own HSA.

You can fund your HSA with pretax dollars and spend them tax-free on qualifying medical expenses. The best part of an HSA is that the funds you contribute roll over year to year. So, if you start contributing prior to retirement, you can potentially reduce your taxable income while saving for retirement medical expenses.

Of course, it's important to review whether or not high-deductible insurance meets your needs adequately.

If you frequently see the doctor or have an ongoing medical condition where you'd benefit from a lower annual deductible or out-of-pocket maximum, a high-deductible health plan may not be right for you.

Retirement Income Randall

Randall knew that between his wife and himself, they had several ways that they would be receiving income in retirement. Unfortunately, he wasn't entirely clear on where that income was coming from—and how much each source would provide over the course of their retirement. He decided to sit down with a fee-only[8] financial advisor to crunch the numbers.

First and foremost, Randall had a 401k through his employer. He had been steadily saving for the past 30 years and was proud to have a balance of close to $1 million in his account. His wife, Sandra, had no 401k through her small business employer but had saved an additional $400,000 in her traditional IRA. Neither Randall nor Sandra had a Roth IRA as part of their portfolio.

Through his employer, Randall was eligible to receive a pension. He had originally planned on pursuing a joint-and-survivor option but was now considering taking the lump sum and having his fee-only

---

8   A fee-only financial advisor is compensated only with fees their clients pay. They do not receive compensation from the sale of financial products.

advisor help him reinvest the funds to better align with his retirement-lifestyle goals. Finally, both he and his wife were set to receive Social Security, since they would start taking their benefits at full retirement age. So Randall and his wife would be receiving income from:

1. His 401k

2. Her traditional IRA

3. His pension

4. Their collective Social Security benefits

All told, Randall and his advisor set out to pursue a goal of having 80 percent of their current monthly income distributed to them through various channels throughout retirement.

Working with an Advisor

Working with a fee-only financial planner can help you to understand not only how much you need to have saved to retire and live comfortably but also the best way to organize your savings for an income during retirement.

My job as an advisor is to help people run the numbers and determine whether their dream retirement lifestyle is in reach. If it's not, I can help them determine what changes to make either in their savings, work plans, or retirement-lifestyle goals to still retire comfortably. If you're struggling with the financial stumbling blocks of retirement planning, reaching out to a professional can help.

Chapter 12

HEALTH CARE IN RETIREMENT

Stumbling Block #8: You're Not Sure How to Access Health Care in Retirement

According to a Fidelity survey,[9] retired couples over age 65 could need an average of $295,000 saved for health care costs in retirement! Unfortunately, that number shows no sign of going down in the near future. It's natural that, as we age, more and more of our budget will get eaten up with health-related expenses.

---

9 "Planning for Health Care Costs in Retirement," Fidelity, accessed February 6, 2021, https://institutional.fidelity.com/app/item/RD_13569_42402/retirement-planning-health-care-costs.html.

No person is 100 percent immune to the health concerns that come with aging. Even if you've led a relatively healthy life, other factors can affect you as you move through retirement. Your family history, for example, often plays a large role. You may also find that physical health isn't as much of a concern as mental health.

Every year, there are approximately 10 million new cases of dementia reported.[10] Individuals who lose their memory and the ability to care for themselves often incur additional medical costs and may even end up paying for a long-term care facility or memory center.

I'm not saying any of this to scare you. Quite the opposite, in fact. The more you are cognizant of the potential health care costs associated with retirement, the better you can prepare ahead of time. Our holistic health is one of the largest factors that plays into our overall quality of life and happiness. If you're planning your ideal retirement, you need to be thinking about how you're going to pay for the health care you need!

Retirement Stepping-Stone #8: Explore Your Options and Know When to Enroll

A good first step in thinking about paying for medical expenses in retirement is to determine what type of

---

10   "Dementia," World Health Organization, September 21, 2020, https://www.who.int/news-room/fact-sheets/detail/dementia.

health care coverage will work best for you and how you plan to pay for it. Check first with your employer. For example, a huge employer in my area of Ohio is Marathon Petroleum.

Currently, Marathon offers health insurance to retirees through the company's preferred providers—Anthem BlueCross BlueShield and Express Scripts. This is an excellent option because the cost is typically lower than Medicare premiums, and it allows previous Marathon employees to maintain the coverage they're accustomed to.

However, for most people, employers don't continue to offer insurance after retirement. If this describes you, your primary option will be to pursue Medicare. Unfortunately, many retirees are unsure how Medicare works. Let's review the different parts of Medicare and how you can leverage them to minimize medical costs in retirement.

Medicare Overview

Medicare is composed of four parts—A, B, C, and D. Each offers a different type of coverage. According to www.Medicare.gov, Part A generally covers:

- Inpatient care in a hospital
- Skilled-nursing facility care

- Nursing-home care (inpatient care in a skilled nursing facility that's not custodial or long-term care)

- Hospice care

- Home health care

Think of Part A as the most basic type of coverage available. It covers some costs in a worst-case or extreme scenario where you need expensive care.

Part B covers "medically necessary" and "preventive" services. This could mean inpatient or outpatient mental-health expenses, well-patient visits, nonelective surgeries, and other medical services. Typically, when people think of Medicare, they're thinking of Parts A and B combined. These are the parts of Medicare that people most commonly enroll in.

While Parts A and B can both be beneficial, they won't always provide the same level of coverage that you're used to before retirement. This is where Parts C and D come into play. Medicare Part C, or Medicare Advantage Plans, include both HMO (health maintenance organization) and PPO (preferred provider organization) options.

Medicare Part C is offered through third-party, private insurance providers. Retirees who choose to enroll in a Medicare Advantage Plan do so because they are looking for specific additional coverage to supplement what is available through traditional Medicare Parts A and B.

Finally, Part D is prescription or drug coverage. There are several different Part D plans available, and retirees should be careful when selecting the plan they enroll in. Some plans will cover specific prescription drugs or brands, while others may not.

Long-Term Care Insurance and Planning for Hefty Expenses

Although Medicare offers some coverage for long-term care or other medically necessary care, the reality is that long-term care is often required as you age. However, enrolling in long-term care insurance in your mid- to late 50s could mean pricey premiums that aren't within your retirement budget.

Many people who don't feel long-term care insurance is affordable or necessary instead choose to self-insure. In other words, they carve out a portion of their portfolio that remains "untouchable" except for medical expenses. A good rule of thumb is to plan for a worst-case scenario and save accordingly. Once these funds are set aside and earmarked for medical expenses, you can allocate the funds in the account so that they gain a small amount of interest in low-risk investment vehicles.

The possibility of your needing the funds from this account now or in early retirement is low. Your health will likely stay relatively good or at least consistent during your initial 5–15 years of retirement. Because of this, having your funds continue to grow and earn interest helps you to increase the amount of your self-insurance nest egg to use later on in your 80s or 90s.

Health Savings Accounts

Another way to offset the costs of medical expenses in retirement is to start putting funds aside to cover smaller expenses—like prescription costs and co-pays. If you are currently enrolled in a High Deductible Health Plan, you might consider opening up a Health Savings Account (HSA). All contributions to your HSA are pretax. In other words, they lower your taxable income when you contribute.

Unlike Flexible Savings Accounts (which have similar principles), your HSA's balance carries over from year to year. So, you could feasibly contribute up to the government-allowed maximum each year and carry those contributions into retirement as a medical-expense fund.

Keep in mind that funds in your HSA can only be used for qualifying medical expenses. If you're ever uncertain about whether or not an expense qualifies, I recommend you look up the list of HSA-approved expenses on the IRS website.

Healthy Heather

Heather has always been in good health, even as she's aged. Years ago she ran marathons as a hobby and still enjoys meeting up with her long-distance running group a few times a week to log some miles. She regularly attends yoga classes and has focused on cleaning up her diet in recent years. However, Heather knows that there's a history of dementia in her family. She decided to schedule an appointment with her general practitioner to talk through preventive wellness.

One thing her doctor mentioned was that many individuals with dementia or Alzheimer's disease end up requiring assisted living in their later years. Even if they're physically healthy, it becomes challenging for them to manage daily life without help. Heather knew this to be true, having watched her mother go through the process of moving into assisted living after her father could no longer solely manage her care.

Instead of being fearful of assisted living (and the associated costs), Heather decided to do some research. There were several residences in her area that offered memory care. There were also a few retirement communities with options for assisted living and memory care as residents aged. Knowing her options ahead of time should they become necessary allows her to make empowered decisions about her lifestyle and health in retirement, to get a financial estimate for what assisted living might cost—and how to save accordingly.

Planning Ahead for a Happy and Healthy Retirement

Your health is the foundation of everything else in your life. Without your health, you won't be able to enjoy the retirement you've worked so hard to build. This is why it's so important to prioritize your health in your retirement budget. By setting funds aside to ensure your needs are met, you're setting up a lifestyle that will work for you regardless of the health problems you may or may not face.

Chapter 13

EXPLORING PLAN B

Stumbling Block #9: You Don't Love Your Retirement Lifestyle

Have you read this far and still feel uncomfortable with the concept of retirement?

You're not alone!

The truth is that traditional retirement isn't for everyone. Some people feel nervous about retiring before they take the leap. Others don't realize until after they've already left their jobs that they don't like the lifestyle they've built.

Regardless of how much effort you put into planning your dream retirement, you may still find that you don't love it once you're living it every day. Many retirees end up feeling like they need something more to fill their time after retirement, even if they had already planned several fulfilling activities to pursue.

Retirement Stepping-Stone #9: Have a Backup Plan

This is why it's critical to have a Plan B in place. I don't mean to say that you have to rush back to work at the first sign of feeling unfulfilled. Quite the opposite, in fact. Having a Plan B simply means that you have come up with a backup plan in case your original idea for retirement doesn't pan out the way you had imagined.

Not sure what a Plan B looks like in practice? Let's look at a few examples based on real-life retirees I know.

Dan the Dentist

Dan had been a dentist for more than 30 years. He ran his own practice and loved his work. However, as retirement neared, he knew that he didn't want the continued stress of maintaining his own practice—even if he wasn't the primary dentist in the office anymore. So Dan lined up a buyer for his business. One of the newer dentists on staff was ready to dive in headfirst, and Dan knew he could trust him with his clients and his legacy.

Dan's original retirement plan was to spend more time with his family and to be a snowbird in Florida for half of the year. He had spent a lot of years working long hours to grow his business and was ready for a well-deserved break. However, as an entrepreneur, Dan also knew he liked to keep busy. He was a bit worried about feeling like he had nothing to do in retirement—even if his schedule was full of the hobbies and people he loved.

Dan created a Plan B that fit his needs. He would take two years completely off—just enjoying retirement to the fullest. After that, if he was starting to feel bored, Dan would pivot to pursue a career as a professor. He had always enjoyed teaching and training new dentists on his staff and thought he might be interested in doing that full or part time.

Dan ended up pursuing teaching sooner than expected. An opportunity opened up, and he jumped at the chance to do something he loved.

Margaret the Maker

Margaret was about to retire from her long career as a successful paralegal. She had always enjoyed her job but felt like it lacked the creativity she craved. Margaret was looking forward to retiring in the traditional way. She and her husband were downsizing their home and purchasing an RV to travel the country just as they'd always wanted.

Still, Margaret felt like her lifelong desire to pursue creativity might not be fulfilled by her Plan A (travel). Margaret's Plan B was to pick up a new creative hobby—crocheting—while on the road.

Crocheting was not something Margaret had ever done in the past, but her daughter told her that she could help set up a shop on a site like Etsy.com to make a little bit of money selling her work on the side. It may be that Margaret chooses to crochet for fun, but she loved the fact that she has a Plan B in place in case she decides to pursue the craft after retiring.

Vick the Volunteer

Vick didn't have a Plan B heading into retirement. He was ready to simply enjoy long days fishing, reading books, and spending time with his grandkids. However, when his wife passed away a few years before retirement, Vick became more heavily involved in his local faith community.

One day, his lead pastor asked Vick if he'd be interested in volunteering on the OWL (Older, Wiser, Livelier) board. This group helps run events and makes decisions about how the organization gets involved in the local community. Although a nearly full-time volunteer position hadn't been in Vick's plans, he was excited to pursue this unexpected opportunity. It became his Plan B.

Creating Your Plan B

While many retirees are like Vick and are lucky enough to have a Plan B fall into their laps, it's wise to have a set plan (or two!) in place in case your Plan A doesn't turn out to be personally fulfilling. When creating a Plan B, here are some things to consider:

- What hobbies do you have?

- How do you like to spend your time?

- What unique skills do you possess?

- What opportunities may be available for you to pivot to during retirement?

- Who do you want to spend your time with?

- What activities energize you and bring you joy?

The goal of your Plan B may not be to fill 100 percent of your time. Instead it should offer a unique way to settle in and truly enjoy your time as a retiree if your original retirement plan doesn't turn out the way you had hoped.

Chapter 14

TAKING THE LEAP AND LEAVING A LEGACY

Stumbling Block #10: You Want to Make an Impact Beyond Your Retirement Years

The final stumbling block retirees encounter is how to make an impact beyond their own lives. For many, raising a family and having enjoyed a career they're passionate about is a legacy in itself. I don't want to discount that. But some retirees want to do more; they want to continue to build a legacy. And I believe that to do that you need to celebrate the steps you've already taken to make an impact on the world around you.

When I think about my mom, I can't help but see the

good she left behind. Through her work raising my sister and me, loving my dad, volunteering through her church, and helping her patients and their families in hospice care, she built a beautiful legacy out of her life. However, I don't think that *she* saw it that way.

After making the transition to retirement, my mom quickly started to feel like her ability to contribute to the world around her had been taken away. She was stressed out about money, and she felt out of place in her own world.

Aging adults who look back on their lives and believe they've had an impact on the world beyond themselves tend to be happier, healthier, and more fulfilled. They age with grace instead of fear or emotional pain.

Retirement Stepping-Stone #10: Create Your Legacy Starting Today

Having a plan in place to both take pleasure in what you've built so far and to continue your legacy during retirement can help you to sidestep negative feelings. Instead, you can transition to a place of joy and personal fulfillment.

Celebrating Your Legacy to Date

Here's where reaching out to your network can be hugely helpful. Whether you're someone who enjoys being the center of attention or not, I recommend taking the time to focus on yourself and asking others to help you celebrate your life to date.

This could take the form of a retirement party, or it could be a birthday celebration shortly after you retire. Or it could simply mean having your close family or friends over for dinner or reaching out to them to talk over the phone. Your goal should be twofold:

- To celebrate your move to this next chapter of life—you've earned it!

- To gather objective information from others about how you've impacted them personally or how they view your legacy.

Most people struggle to see their own value. Even if you're a confident person, you often don't see how your life or your work impacts the lives of others. What may be a regular Tuesday for you may be the light bulb moment that inspired someone else to carry on your legacy of being more giving, loving, or passionate about their work.

Asking those you trust to help you see your legacy or to celebrate it with you can be an eye-opening experience. It doesn't have to feel like an attention grab, either! You can humbly ask your loved ones to walk this journey with you and tell them that this is part of you understanding your legacy more deeply so you can continue to build it in the years to come.

Not comfortable reaching out to others?

You can also choose to celebrate your legacy alone, though you may lack the insight of others. If you choose to go this route, take your time to think about:

- How you've impacted the lives around you

- What accomplishments you're most proud of (raising a family, building a rock-solid marriage, creating an internship program at work or in your community, and so on)

- How those accomplishments make you feel and why

- How you'd like to see that legacy continued in the future—possibly even beyond your own life

Setting Up Next Steps

Your legacy doesn't have to end with you. Many retirees are uncomfortable thinking about the inevitability that we will all pass away at some point. However, I firmly believe that if you embrace building a legacy and using your unique skills to impact others beyond your lifetime, you will be infinitely more fulfilled both now and in the future.

After all, you have spent a lifetime pursuing your dreams, guiding and teaching others, and following what you're most passionate about. Why should that end with you?

Take time to think about what next steps you want to take to continue your legacy—even beyond your lifetime. This may have a financial component. For example, if you're passionate about impacting the lives of others through your chosen career as a teacher, you might look for ways to set up support for future generations of educators. This could translate into budgeting for a scholarship fund at your local college or university or setting up a mentorship program in the school district where you taught.

Don't be afraid to think outside of the box; brainstorm several ideas that feel right to you. You can always pursue more than one path to building your legacy. If you're feeling overwhelmed, remember this: Your legacy can also be carried forward by the people you love.

When I consider my mom's life, I see a strong woman who left a lasting legacy, whether she intended to or not. She may not have seen her impact before she passed away, but my family, friends, community, and I all see it today.

In many ways, I view this book as part of her legacy. I know that, as someone with a truly giving and nurturing heart, she would have wanted me to reach out to others and to help them build a life and a retirement they love.

She would have wanted her experience and story to help others see that retirement is more than just dollars and cents—it's about finding and pursuing your passion during a new chapter of life.

Retirement planning means having your finances and your personal lifestyle plan both nailed down before taking the leap. Leaving a legacy is the ultimate way of achieving a fulfilling retirement and, by extension, a fulfilling life.

CONCLUSION

You've now successfully walked through all 10 retirement stumbling blocks and have started to turn them into stepping-stones! The fact that you've read this far shows me that you're ready to tackle your retirement journey, and I commend you for that.

Let's review the ten stepping-stones as you begin your retirement planning journey:

1. Take the time to explore your purpose and your values heading into retirement. Getting clear about how you want to live your life according to what matters most to you can help you plan for a fulfilling next chapter.

2. Don't be afraid to dream big! Reviewing all of your ideas for what retirement could be can help you to clarify exactly what kind of lifestyle you want—even if you have to edit some of it down due to financial restrictions later on.

3. Plan for your daily life. Bucket-list items are wonderful, and you've certainly earned the opportunity to pursue them. But having a loose idea of how you'd like to spend a random Tuesday morning can help to steer your path and ensure that you don't wind up bored, unfulfilled, or depressed.

4. Focus on building your social circle before retirement or immediately after retiring. Connect with family and friends, and even consider finding other retirees who share your interests to spend time with.

5. Building toward big lifestyle changes slowly can help you adjust to anything new (a big move, downsizing your home, and so on) before making the transition to retirement. It can also help to highlight whether certain retirement dreams are a fit for your unique personality and needs. Consider downsizing in advance of retirement, test-driving relocation, and incorporating elements of a lifestyle change into your daily life before leaving your job.

6. Create a retirement budget with the goal of your wealth outliving you. This might mean adjusting your lifestyle expectations or working with a fee-only financial advisor to build a strategy that addresses your needs.

7. Take the time to gain a deeper understanding of how you will create your income in retirement. You could leverage savings, Social Security, your pension, and other sources to create cash flow to sustain your lifestyle.

8. Figure out a plan for health care before entering retirement. Whether you are looking to enroll in Medicare, leverage an HSA for health costs, or continue to get access to health care through your employer in retirement, knowing this in advance can save you a lot of headache down the line. Your goal should be to retire with confidence and to "button up" any questions (including health care) before taking the leap.

9. Think through a backup plan. What will you do if you don't enjoy being retired? Have a few ideas in mind in case the retirement lifestyle you've teed up for yourself isn't one that ends up fulfilling you.

10. Imagine the type of legacy you want to leave. Many people think of legacy as something that

magically happens after they pass away. That couldn't be further from the truth! You start building your legacy in life through your actions and words. How do you want to lean into build your legacy and make an impact in retirement?

I know that retirement planning can feel overwhelming, but by focusing on just one stepping-stone at a time, you can build a lifestyle that's fulfilling as you make this transition.

Working on this book has helped me reflect on the events of March, 22, 2011, and how they have impacted my life. As I've pored over these pages, seeking to tell my mom's story, I've become ever more committed to conveying what I've learned to you, the reader.

One parting piece of advice I'd like to give you is this—remember that you don't have to do this alone.

Retirement planning is stressful in the best of circumstances. Hiring a professional fiduciary financial planner means that you'll have someone on your side who has your best interests at heart.

If you're looking to learn more about financial planning, I encourage you to reach out to a fee-only financial advisor or my team at Hixon Zuercher Capital Management (https://hzcapital.com). Although we're based in Findlay, Ohio, we fully utilize technology to serve clients around the country. Our firm specializes in retirement-planning services, and we've helped hundreds of clients transition from successful careers into the retirement they've always dreamed of.

I'm so proud of all the work you're putting into building your dream retirement! Together, I know we can make your plan reflect your values, address your concerns, and create a lifestyle you love.

EPILOGUE

I believe the saying *time heals all wounds* is pretty accurate. A decade has distanced the pain of what happened that fateful day on March 22, 2011. Yet, like tossing a stone into a still lake, the ripple effects are still there. The wife, mother, and grandma that Pam Hixon was changed the course of history for my family.

The members of my family have each worked to turn our tragedy into triumph and our personal stumbling blocks into stepping-stones. With every passing day, we still miss Mom, but we've learned to move on and pick up where she left off—to try to help others, to encourage those around us, and to continue her legacy.

My dad officially retired from his factory job in March 2014, three years after Mom's passing. His passion for farming, however, is something he'll never retire from. He runs a 160-acre grain and livestock farm in the same house he and Mom built.

He married again on December 7, 2013, and his wife, Pat, has quickly become a loved and important part of our family.

My sister, Net, and her husband, Mark, reside on a farm outside of Mt. Cory, Ohio, and they both have businesses to run. Net pays homage to Mom throughout her home and garden with many butterfly images that symbolize their mother-daughter bond. For Net, losing Mom was devastating, but she has surrounded herself with a strong network of friends, and she strives to build a good relationship with my kids by being the "cool aunt."

My wife, Keri, valiantly supported me as I dealt with my grief. I don't know a stronger woman. I can't conceive of a better soul mate. While struggling herself to come to terms with my mom's choice, she was able to help our kids understand what happened. Today Keri is primarily a stay-at-home mom. She loves to work in her garden and, most importantly, love and support our kids.

Our oldest, Eliana, was four years old when her Mama Pam died, and she has the most memories of her. Eliana enjoys playing piano and has the gift of a beautiful voice. She has a tender heart that reminds me of Mom in the way she cares for others.

Kya, who was just three years old at the time, has only faint memories of her grandmother. She's the funniest kid I know, with a cadence of comedy that has me laughing till I cry. I can picture her making Mama Pam laugh for hours if they had a chance to hang out together.

As you may recall, Keri was seven months pregnant with our son, Everett, when Mom died, so they never met. He's now in the fourth grade and dreams of playing football. I know Mom would have supported him whatever his goals, and I can't help but wonder if he would've been the miracle that Mom needed to dig out of her slump. Meeting her first and only grandson might have been just what the doctor ordered.

As for me, I hadn't visited Mom's grave since we laid her to final rest back in 2011. I can't quite articulate why. Maybe I've been busy. Maybe I don't like cemeteries. Maybe since she chose to leave us, I just couldn't muster the willpower to go and say hi.

Writing this book, however, has been cathartic. A few weeks ago, I made my first visit. I brought two things with me: flowers and the draft manuscript of this book. That seemed particularly appropriate.

Her story brought me to this point, and I thought giving her a first glimpse of the result of my path might make her proud. I picture her telling me it was the best book she'd ever read. She asks me to sign it—the first autographed copy.

I oblige:

To Mom,
The best mom a son could ask for . . .

Love always, Tony

Moments pass. The sun peeks through a cloud. My visit has come to an end. I'll be back, though. I'll let her know the impact she had on others by those who take action as a result of reading this book. I'll let her know that the proceeds from the sale of this book go to the Pamela M. Hixon Memorial Scholarship Fund that Keri and I set up in Mom's memory at the University of Findlay.

Each year, the scholarship goes to a worthy nursing student with good grades and financial need. Mom would be proud, I know. Every year, I meet the scholarship recipient. I tell them the story behind the award and encourage them on their path in the health care industry. These students are deserving, hardworking, and hopeful. I'm reminded that the future is bright.

I'm reminded that the best is ahead.

ABOUT THE AUTHOR

TONY HIXON is a cofounder and chief operating officer of Hixon Zuercher Capital Management. He has been providing financial advice to his firm's clients since 2003. After having tragically lost his mom, he approaches financial advice in a different way. "I firmly believe that our clients aren't served when we look only at the numbers," he says. The entire Hixon Zuercher team focuses on a holistic approach when working with pre-retiree clients, because they've seen firsthand the effects of not having a plan to live a values-based life throughout retirement.

Tony says, "If finances are the only thing we consider, we overlook the well-being of our clients and the long-term satisfaction they'll receive from having a financial plan in place."

To continue the conversation, visit www.tonyhixon.com where you can subscribe to his weekly blog, connect with him on his social media platforms, and download the *Retirement Stepping Stones Workbook*, which serves as a free companion piece to this book. The workbook will elevate your experience and set you on a trajectory of retirement preparedness.

Made in the USA
Middletown, DE
07 July 2023

34682128R00111